AW-10039

hw.design gmbh
Türkenstraße 55 – 57
80799 München

The **World** of
Graphic
Design
at the Galerie von Oertzen

Editors

Klaus Klemp
Olaf Leu
Hans-Christoph von Oertzen

1997
Verlag Hermann Schmidt Mainz

D1734617

"The world of graphic design at the Galerie von Oertzen"
at the Städtische Galerie im Karmeliterkloster,
Frankfurt/Main
from 6 September – 5 October, 1997
and
at the Deutsches Plakatmuseum, Essen
from 26 March – 3 May, 1998

The Gallery

With this catalogue, the Galerie von Oertzen introduces a selection from its comprehensive programme of 40 exhibitions of 16 internationally-renowned graphic designers and design agencies.

Exhibition curators:

Klaus Klemp,
Head of the Office of Culture,
Amt für Wissenschaft und Kunst
der Stadt Frankfurt am Main

Professor Olaf Leu,
Fachhochschule Mainz

Frieder Mellinghoff,
Deutsches Plakatmuseum, Essen

Contents

Klaus Klemp

1 Exhibiting Design

In Germany the engineer rules. Indeed, both in this country and abroad the old prejudice stubbornly remains and sometimes receives an unexpected new boost, or at least so it seems, and even now many people still believe the traditional German virtues of perseverance and attention to practical detail will continue to triumph in the future. The old, established industries are, however, in considerable decline. The production of industrial and consumer goods, as we read in the newspapers every day, is shifting more and more to Eastern Europe and Southeast Asia, as a progressive internationalizing of production is brought about by ever-increasing levels of autximization. CNC-machines are replacing the qualified skilled worker, and on many production lines in Asia today it is not people who control the manufacturing process any more but the computer. The labour cost factor decides the location.

Technology apart, it is more and more the design of a product that determines the ability to compete, so it is not always the unidimensional aesthetic of function which decides marketing strategy or acceptance in the market place. The Italian furniture and interior designers demonstrated that in the Eighties. Whether something is accepted or not does not depend solely on its ease of use but also involves a strong emotional component, and the same goes to a considerable degree for American graphic design in the Sixties. Here again, the so-called functional rules and norms were nearly completely abandoned, even to some extent frowned upon. This escape from the artistic restrictions of pure logic was fun for the consumer and reader and they rewarded it generously. Human beings, though blessed with the gift of reason, do not want to be reduced to that alone; rationality is always only one side of a much more complex person, of which a large part is occupied by sentiment and subjectivity. At the height of the second industrial revolution, producers and designers already understood the significance of the impact their products made on the senses.

"The idea that it is quite enough for the engineer that a building, an implement or a machine he has invented fulfils a purpose, is wrong; even worse is the remark, often heard nowadays, that if it fulfils a purpose it must at the same time be beautiful."

Hermann Muthesius, 1909

From about the end of the 17th century, art and technology went their separate ways, so it was out of the first industrial revolution of the steam engine, of heavy industry and the mass production of goods for consumption, together with the industrialisation of printing and the mass circulation of newspapers and posters, that evolved what we today call design. It was a long and painful, sometimes successful, sometimes rather barren, attempt to achieve a creative form which coincided with the spirit of the times and the requirements of civilisation.

The development of design was accompanied by public showings and subsequent debates about the products themselves. Whether at the great world exhibitions in the middle of the 19th century or through the newly-formed trade associations or the emerging museums for design, the champions of the Modern had a very special affinity with the exhibition medium. For example, the first big project of the young Walter Gropius was to organise a building industry exhibition commissioned by the Deutsche Werkbund. In 1930, the magazine "Das Neue Frankfurt" – one of the most important publications on modern design during the interwar years – led a wide-ranging debate on the subject, while the art historian Franz Roh wrote at the time, "one has to expand the opportunities for exhibitions into all fields; the idea of art exhibitions automatically extends to optical creations generally... The most effective intermediary between sensual perception and its physiological abstraction is not the written word but the exhibition."

The important position design exhibitions had achieved during the Weimar Republic was not reached again for a long time after 1945. The economic boom of the Fifties and Sixties largely killed off critical interest in the argument about the new two- and three-dimensional artistic environment. Only in the aftermath of the social upheaval of the mid-Sixties was there

a renewed interest in thinking about contemporary products
and pictures, when both established institutions such as
the Münchner Stadtmuseum and new ones like the Deutsches
Plakatmuseum in Essen initiated an extensive public debate
about the visual phenomena of graphic design.

Things which had previously been of only peripheral
interest now took centre stage: the visual design of public
rooms; the appearance and image of big companies, and the
way state and municipal governments presented themselves to
the people, and so on. This change was accompanied by a wider
appreciation of the international scene as the economically
more robust Bundesrepublik overcame the Neo-Biedermeier
tastes of the Adenauer era and increasingly opened itself up
to outside, mainly Anglo-American, influences. Magazines such
as "Twen", designed by Willi Fleckhaus, created a new zest for
life, and ideas that had at first appealed chiefly to pop music
and youth culture rapidly gained ground in the areas of company
advertising and corporate design.

However, it was not only the big exhibition houses, the
printing media and televison that changed the visual parame-
ters; many smaller, mainly private, initiatives also contributed
a great deal to the process. Among these was the Galerie
von Oertzen in Frankfurt am Main, which since 1984 has dedicated itself consistently to international graphic design.
Anybody who suspects there may be a commercial venture
behind this gallery is both right and wrong. VON OERTZEN GmbH
is a traditional but technologically modern company in the
pre-press sector, but the "Galerie von Oertzen" is the combined
love- and brain-child of Hans-Christoph von Oertzen, which
has not earned its owner a penny. Long in collaboration with
the Frankfurt designer and promoter Olaf Leu, this company
gallery has produced over the last twelve years an exhibition
programme that would do credit to many design museums.

The Galerie von Oertzen was and is the most sought-after
address for all insiders and followers of graphic design in
the Rhein-Main area and far beyond. The promotional work on
behalf of design quality which has been done there over
a dozen years or so is one reason for this, the other being the
innumerable contacts which have been established over
the years through vernissages, talks and symposia. One simply
cannot praise centres of communication like this too highly,

because it is they who drive the design process forward and make the transition between different styles and generations possible.

The country needs a lot of Galerien von Oertzen.

Hans-Christoph von Oertzen

2

The Gallery, Idea and Reality

The end of the Second World War, which also marked the lifting of the suppression of works of so-called "degenerate art", led to large sections of the German population taking a heightened interest in art and connected activities. The opening up of a world which had for many years been closed for us led to an increased zest for life, and one wanted to meet the artists and share this new beginning with them. My personal interest lay in the setting-up of my own graphics business.

So there grew up in Wiesbaden, where I had fled to from eastern Germany in front of the occupying Soviet forces, a new circle of friends, mainly painters, sculptors, architects and gallery owners. With the encouragement of the Wiesbaden painter, art educationist and gallery owner, Christa Moering, the Galerie von Oertzen was established, and she suggested I should introduce the artists from her circle to the Frankfurt public.

The artist
Christa Moering

In establishing the gallery, I was not thinking of adding another branch to my Frankfurt-based company, which was a publishing and graphics firm. I did not want to be an art dealer. The gallery was intended in the first instance to serve those interested in the artistic events of the day, not only the general public but also employees of the company, who were involved every day in the art of typographic and lithographic design. The idea was to create a meeting and communication centre for all those for whom contemporary art was a major concern. At the same time, it was of course important for me to maintain the image of the company, and the art of the typographer and the lithographer would reach further afield via the gallery.

A start was made in the autumn of 1967 with the Berlin artist Erwin Filter, who had been living in Wiesbaden since the end of the war, followed by Peter Schermuly, Günther Stiller, Hans Laabs and Christa Moering. The circle was quickly enlarged through a friendly connection with the Anglo-African

Ivan Spence, who was based in Ibiza and introduced artists of international standing to the gallery.

However, after the first twelve exhibitions it was clear to me that unless I got involved in the art trade, the gallery could not be made into a success. The exhibiting artists expected sales, especially the ones coming from abroad, some of them from far away, and in any case my own publishing and printing firm was demanding my full personal attention more and more.

I therefore decided to make a pause in all exhibition activities. This lasted until 1984.

In 1983 our graphics firm discontinued metal typesetting and the temptation to make use of the now vacant rooms was so great that I decided to bring the gallery back to life. Meanwhile, the von Oertzen company had sucessfully established itself as a pre-press firm, with an increased number of advertising agencies and big enterprises in industry and trade as clients, so the obvious thing to do was to present examples of top international graphic designs to this new public through exhibitions. It was at this time that I began to work more closely with the successful graphic designer, Professor Olaf Leu, who was famous far beyond the boundaries of the Federal Republic.

Leu was for many years the chairman of the German branch of the Type Director Club of New York and acted as juror in their annual competitions. He was therefore an excellent judge of the international top-design scene, and the prominent position the Galerie von Oertzen came to enjoy as a representative of tip-top international design was mainly thanks to the connections Olaf Leu created for it.

Our personal contacts with artists from four continents – Europe, the Near and Far East, North and South America, and Australia – were a source of great artistic enrichment for the employees of our firm and also of course for the guests, and especially for the students of the nearby colleges. As a result, the gallery won the cooperation of the professors at the Hochschule für Gestaltung in Offenbach am Main and the Fachhochschulen in Darmstadt, Mainz, Wiesbaden and Mannheim in encouraging the students to take part in a workshop with, and arranged by, the designers themselves, on the day after every vernissage. In this way, many personal friendships were formed between the artists, the owner of the gallery and his friends.

Unfortunately, it is not within the scope of this purely
graphic design presentation in the Frankfurt Karmeliterkloster
to introduce more than a section of the forty exhibitions
which the Gallery has offered to the public over the past years.
I have had to do completely without the first part of my
exhibition period from 1967–69 and the 1975 exhibition
of graphics by Max Slevogt, which is in private hands. During
this first exhibition phase, the following artists were introduced
in twelve exhibitions:

Erwin Filter, Germany
Peter Schermuly, Germany
Hans Laabs, Germany
Günther Stiller, Germany
Alberto Gutiérrez, Columbia
Bernhard C. Eder, Austria
Christa Moering, Germany
Eduardo Urculo, Spain
Natale Sapone, Italy
Shiro Sasaki, Japan
Becky Sandstede, Germany
Gisela Aulfes-Daeschler, Germany

Also, from the second exhibition phase from 1984-95,
which included (with a few exceptions) artists and studios
of international graphic design, I can show only fourteen out
of a total of twenty-eight exhibitors. They are:

Anton Stankowski, Germany
Oswaldo Miranda, Brazil
Olaf Leu, Germany
Zdenek Ziegler, Czech Republic
Takenobu Igarashi, Japan
Jean Widmer, France
Gottschalk & Ash Int'l, Switzerland, Canada
Total Design, Holland
Joe Duffy, The Duffy Design Group, USA
Three Australians:
    Ken Cato
    Garry Emery
    Barrie Tucker
Susumu Endo, Japan
Josse Goffin, Belgium
The Partners, England
Yves Zimmermann, Spain

Sadly, we cannot show works from:

Friedrich Poppl, Germany
Mike Rose, Germany
Papier-Ideen, Academy of Fine Arts, Stuttgart, Germany
Henrik Strömberg, Finland
Reiner Seibold, Germany
Zlatko Prica, Croatia
Manfred Kage, Germany
Dietrich Ebert, Germany
Asher Kalderon, Israel
Felipe Taborda, 12 Brazilians, Brazil
Wort-Bild-Wort, TDC New York, USA
Jan Mlodozeniec, Poland
Martin Solomon, USA
Circulo de Creativos Argentinos, Argentina

I am convinced, however, that our selection will give you a good overall picture of what the gallery has been about.

Olaf Leu

3 Graphic Design as material for exhibitions.
The history of "graphic" galleries in Germany.

Introduction:

ICTA – The International Center for the Typographic Arts – was founded in 1961 in New York, mainly on the initiative of Aaron Burns. The idea behind this institution was the world-wide exchange of professional knowledge and design ideas through critical reviews, the discussion of seminal new projects, through publications and exhibitions.

The organisational hub was New York, which in the Six-ties was just at the peak of its creative activity, but it was only decades later that what happened during this period in the field of American Graphic Design became known as "The New Ame-rican School".

ICTA was based on the one hand on the tightly-managed Center in New York, and secondly on the national sections, as they were called, and individual membership.

Over the years, a number of activities developed out of this network which were centrally-organised on one side of the Atlantic – one thinks of the two great world exhibitions of the typographical Arts, "Typomundus 1 and 2" – and which in Euro-pe were arranged by the individual national sections, who were responsible for mounting their own events.

ICTA, membership of which opened up worldwide con-tacts, not only by mail but also at a personal level either through organised visits or informal stays with likeminded souls, was also a conduit to other graphics organisations such as the Art Directors Club and the Type Directors Club of New York, the AIGA, the STD and fellow organisations in Canada, Japan, England and Holland.

It is to the existence of such a worldwide organisation at that time that the galleries in Germany owed their exhibitions pro-gramme and really, through that programme, their own existence.

The story:

In the autumn of 1964, on my first visit to the USA when I was actively pursuing the possibility of an ICTA membership, I was asked to set up a national ICTA section in Germany. We already had several individual memberships in Germany but not our own national section and it was my job as newly-appointed secretary to organise one, under the guidance of Kurt Weidemann. At the time, the membership of the new section was strewn across the whole Republic, so personal meetings were only possible sporadically. Another solution, which might have a much greater impact, would be to install a number of exhibitions which could be made available through the ICTA network.

But where could such exhibitions be held?

At that time, in the early Sixties, I was working for the publicity of the Typo Knauer company in Frankfurt am Main. During my first visit to the USA, I came across some galleries, especially in New York, which had been set up in the working rooms of various firms and fulfilled the function of permanently showing the latest in the field of Graphic Design and also of looking after and extending what one would today call customer contacts, customer services and customer relations. In fact, it was usually the anteroom or vestibule which combined the functions of reception room and gallery in this novel way. The first of these specialised graphic design galleries was "The little Composing Room", situated in New York and founded back in 1921, which was run by Dr Robert Leslie, the owner of Photolettering. I took this gallery idea back with me to Frankfurt and presented it to Heinz Knauer, who then also assigned the double function of reception room and gallery to his own generously-proportioned entrance hall.

In the spring of 1965 the first gallery for Graphic Design in Germany, the Knauer Expo, was opened in the Schleusenstrasse, next to the Frankfurt main-line station, with a presentation of the graphic œuvre of the American, Herb Lubalin. Unfortunately, the ambitious programme of four exhibitions a year lasted only for the first three years and similarly the whole gallery idea survived only until the first economic recession of the early Seventies. In any case, my own withdrawal from exhibition management before this and the unsatisfactory arrangements made to replace me, together with the demise of ICTA itself, meant that all motivation for graphic gallery activities was lost.

Half a year later, in October 1965, the Bauersche Giesserei opened its "galerie bg" at 45 Hamburger Allee with a presentation of the 11th Type Directors Show of New York – this exhibition also came about through the mediation of the ICTA exhibition network.

Frankfurt am Main now had two graphics galleries – Knauer Expo and "galerie bg" – but again they were both destined to enjoy only a few years of activity.

Meanwhile, in the spring of 1966, the idea of a gallery for Graphic Design had been pursued in Munich with the establishment of a second base in Germany called "Intergraphis", situated in the BMW pavilion on the Lenbachplatz. The first presentation here was of the Corporate Design of the Columbia Broadcasting System (CBS) under Lou Dorfsman. However, this large gallery was also granted only a few active years of exhibiting.

In the same year, in the autumn of 1966, an offshoot of the Knauer Expo in Frankfurt emerged in Stuttgart. This was also a vestibule gallery, which brought the original Frankfurt exhibition programme to the Stuttgart public.

1967 also saw the foundation of the third Frankfurt gallery, the Galerie von Oertzen, which, however, presented modern art generally rather than Graphic Design as the subject of its exhibitions and to this extent it was slightly different from the other two galleries.

However, the Galerie von Oertzen records two different periods of exhibiting: modern art from 1967 till 1969, and graphic design from 1984 to the present day.

The early Seventies are synonymous with the dying out of all exhibition activities throughout the (then still divided) Republic. Only at the beginning of the Eighties was there a rekindling of the old idea of the mid-Sixties. One reason for this renewal was the activity of the Studio für Typographie und Reprosatz, Schumacher-Gebler, in Munich, which in the following years managed to produce something that could be described as consistent exhibition work – without calling it a gallery – while on the other hand it was due to the determined maintenance of gallery activity by the von Oertzen exhibitions centre, which remains the only gallery for Graphic Design to survive in the city of Frankfurt am Main.

Summary:

With the exception of "Intergraphis", it was firms in the pre-press sector which had committed themselves to gallery activity. Founded by private initiative, they were of course dependent on economic swings, so it is no wonder if one speaks of them today in the past tense. The exception is the Galerie von Oertzen. On reflection, the interesting fact is that all of the first presentations, such as the two Knauer Expos, Intergraphis and "galerie bq", covered American material and it was by these routes that the "New American School" found its way to Germany.

Friedrich Friedl

4 Contribution to the exhibition
catalogue

Let's get to the point.

In our century the development of graphic design has
made enormous progress in quantity and quality. At the same
time there has been a radical change in the design profession:
the move away from poster painting to commercial art, then to
graphic design and finally to visual communication was accompanied, and even to a great extent triggered, by fundamental
technical changes, by refinements in the way we look at shape,
by a broadening of conceptual thinking.

The fact that the current situation of graphic art in the
metropolitan cities allows the relics of past fashions in design
to be revived can be refreshing for one observer and a source of
irritation to another, can be defined as enrichment or regression, and thought of as a search for alternatives or a sign of the
bankruptcy of our current ideas. Being clear about the meaning
of the myriad forms of appearance that design can take, and
their objective or personal appraisal, does not require inspired
instinct on the one hand or just leaving nature to evolve a solution on the other but intensive debate leading to sound practical
and theoretical conclusions.

A sober stock-taking shows that, in spite of wonderful
developments in design, we are confronted at the end of our
century with the same problems as at the beginning: it was the
yearning after private mythologies and touching romantic
hopes that motivated Art Nouveau and it still drives the present.
This rebellion, which breezily calls for the applied designer to be
both an independent artist and his own patron, is a product of
present day intellectual confusion and is more of a self-admiring
exhibitionism, striking hackneyed avantgarde poses, than a
seriously thought-out position in the field of graphic communication. The evermore increasingly conventional "unconventional"
attitude in design and the yearning for free expression is no sub-
stitute for recognizing the need for serious visual communication.

To a remarkable and increasing degree, the skills which, now as always, lead to this most important goal in applied design are being acquired less and less often, partly as a consequence of their unfailingly superficial treatment by teachers in the Hochschulen, partly because of the increasing devaluation of visual symbols through overuse and partly as a result of enthusiastic, even semi-religious conferences and other forms of art tourism. For the culture industry this is no reason to stop endlessly throwing new design stars into the consumer circusring by introducing new forms, which are for the most part however not new forms, by publishing books totally devoid of intelligence and by organising "exhibitions" to objectify these airy nothings. All this is just registering the facts, not complaining about them, because the art world has probably always been like that, but the reason for pointing these things out is to encourage the proactive seeking out of positive changes and improvements, in many different directions, by means of sound theoretical and practical procedures and research.

As it is, knowledge of the different forms used in graphic art is being built up piecemeal from the accidental discoveries of amateur enthusiasts: here a leaflet attracts attention, there a poster, a plastic bag, a television spot. From these objects come exhibitions in the cultural world, mostly held in museums of commercial art, which illustrate historical developments leading neatly up to the present and pour out a soft-hearted, woolly-minded futurism on lavender-scented paper: this is the work of artified private individuals who are without relevance and have no acquaintance with the profession at all. It is true that some regions have technical museums. The Rhein-Main area boasts international attractions such as the Gutenberg-Museum in Mainz and the Klingspor-Museum in Offenbach, in which the whole development of craft and design is fully documented, and there are always repeated private efforts to generate interest, or rather business, in graphic design. Poster shops and the antiquarian departments of bookshops, for example, have seized on this opportunity for their own benefit, but rarely with success and rarely with knowledge of or bearing on the design professions.

However, through the growing appreciation of creative graphic design new forums have emerged for a continuing debate at a professional level. One of the most remarkable European galleries for graphic design, which has set international standards since 1972, is the print gallery of Pieter Brattinga in Amsterdam. Over the years, exhibitions have been mounted there of projects by the most influential graphic designers, whom Brattinga, with a sure eye for quality, often discovered before they became famous. The gallery was conceived as a complement to his graphic design agency.

Since 1984, the Galerie von Oertzen in Frankfurt has achieved the same importance and widespread recognition, but using a different concept. Occupying the working rooms of a highly technical "Full-Service" company for the combined text and picture communications media, which has been successful right across regional borders, the gallery presents an interesting symbiosis of classical and contemporary craftsmanship but it has also taken on the cultural mission of not only showing the best international graphic products but also letting them be actively experienced.

These cultural events in the graphics field, which have in each case provided a coordinated pattern of outstanding exhibitions, with carefully-researched and illuminating opening speeches and opportunities for contact with the participating designers, all in the presence of design specialists and members of the firm's staff, have been exceptionally positively and actively received by a widely interested public in the Rhein-Main area. The workshops that are organised, with the collaboration of the various designers, for the day after the opening are as good as having lecturers visiting the Hochschulen because they provide the opportunity, especially for Visual Communication students from Darmstadt, Mainz, Offenbach and Wiesbaden, to study and discuss both the design and the designer at close hand.

When one considers that the best designers from Brazil, Japan, France, Poland, England and Germany have been invited and exhibited, one can sense what continuity of quality one has been able to experience here, and what effect these activities have had on the professional design scene throughout the region and beyond. The Galerie von Oertzen deserves our gratitude for promoting professional quality within the design culture.

Frieder Mellinghoff

5 | Background

Throughout his career, company owner Hans-Christoph von Oertzen has adopted a system of work that enables him to fit several different areas of activity together at once. Basically, this mental complexity is business-orientated, but the choice of area in which to develop his business successfully was made on entirely personal grounds: after the Second World War his private ambition was to devote himself to the visual arts, to bring creative works to the notice of others and at the same time to use this interest as an opportunity to bring people together socially.

We discover art through encountering individual works and their creators, but also through social gatherings with friends who draw inspiration and understanding from the contemplation of colour and form. What is so special in this case is that although in familiar circles like this everybody trusts each other and is happily aware of a community of interest, nevertheless a certain tolerance is also demanded because one's own ego is inevitably differentiated from others. From the beginning therefore social activity was considered not an end in itself but more like a discreet school of manners which could be carried over into everyday business life. On top of that, both the inspiring ability of artists to pursue an independent line and the aesthetic training which encourages it held a certain fascination for this generation, which identified strongly with the qualities of courage, strength and willingness to take risks. The circle of friends in Wiesbaden to which Hans-Christoph belonged could justly claim a share in all these values.

This philanthropic, idealistic beginning was confronted after a few years with two trends which forced decisions to be made: first of all, the expansion of commercial dealing in works of art by our city galleries exerted pressure from outside, while secondly the growth of the von Oertzen company itself, which serviced the print communication trade, demanded a concen-

tration on purely business matters from inside. Eventually –
after a few years when exhibiting was completely suspended –
came the synthesis from the USA, brought over by Olaf Leu.
He had noticed on the other side of the Atlantic how cleverly
modern print production studios dealt with the subject of
graphic design, how as a qualitative extra they arranged the
aesthetic components of commissioned work into themes
in small in-company exhibitions and put first-class potential
on show.

This system blended in perfectly with the ethos of the
von Oertzen company and on top of that revealed a number of
potential business advantages. Presenting top quality typographic and iconographic design in a newly-restored Galerie von
Oertzen, with the aim of communicating both information and
a sense of values, was absolutely in accordance with the goals
the owner had set himself. It involves all the employees in a
scrutiny of everything to do with up-to-date graphic forms of
expression. It points to wider horizons. It provides the opportunity to share a sense of joy and admiration, again in a social
context, with friends of the house, with clients and with other
interested visitors. It communicates a feeling of expectation,
as though a Guild of Creative Adventurers were opening up a
New World.

Hans-Christoph plays a specially important role in his
capacity as host. First, he invites the designers of the works
that are being exhibited to a lively "baptism", where often
a work specially developed by the artist for the Galerie
von Oertzen will then receive, as "work in process", its finishing
touches on one of the gallery's printing presses. And finally he
brings the designers together with young people who are still
in education and want to try to follow in the footsteps of the
great masters. Anyone can see for himself that such a stimulat-
ing wellspring of opinion and experience is the "hottest tip"
on the regional scene and, as such, also fulfils the business
purpose of attracting both new clients and highly-motivated
employees of the future.

The choice of works he has exhibited is international and
targeted. Anton Stankowski, for example, is a creative designer
who found his aesthetic regeneration over decades of exploring
the path between pictorial art and functional commercial graphics. As a supporter of the Bauhaus he built bridges between
the two disciplines and demonstrated how an artist achieves

the absolute of a form in his pictures and how a designer makes this visual effect usable in everyday communication. The economy of means was always an important aspect of this process, for by weaving both traditions together into a single, stronger texture he gave the company a commercial edge and in doing so underwrote Hans-Christoph von Oertzen's deeper aims. During this process of development, Stankowski's trade marks and symbols became the obvious way to look at things for everyone; however, exhibiting within the company revealed a much wider palette and demonstrated from what rich aesthetic experimental data he had drawn his designs.

Literally from another world came the works of Takenobu Igarashi, who had been using CAD for years and was most at home developing typographic pictures out of it. The basis for these pictures was mainly of course the "western style" alphabet, but out of that he constructed three-dimensional forms which came close to the ideogrammatic origins of Chinese and Japanese writing. At the same time, through this technical concept he was pointing to the relationship between word and space, to the fact that every message has to cross space and that his own three-dimensional word pictures were designed to appear as volumes occupying space.

Exhibiting tables of numbers pictured in the MOMA calendars for different years, a project agreed upon for six years with the Museum of Modern Art in New York but later extended to ten, was significant in terms of cultural history. Its aim was a contest between man and machine, the graphic designer and the computer. For ten years, there appeared twelve monthly sheets of dates, none of which was allowed a twin. (Nature is merciful!) To cogitate on these intellectual and experimental dimensions of graphic design, and typography in particular, was an object lesson for all who were allowed to look and listen!

While other firms gave up exhibition activities of this kind after a time, for Hans-Christoph von Oertzen the principles behind his gallery project were so important and the positive response to his efforts altogether so satisfying, that he refused to succumb to the widespread symptoms of fatigue. In cooperation with Olaf Leu he integrated into his firm a testing ground which, especially in these years when technological communication is advancing across a wide front, remains excitingly at the interface between tradition and innovation.

It is undoubtedly a work of art in itself not to let such activities become a commercial burden, but it would be disastrous to leave these accumulated experiences only for the academics to theorize over in abstracto.

As a result of his imaginative conceptual framework, Hans-Christoph von Oertzen has created a new dimension of social significance. We should examine very closely what is happening there, we should thank him for his enlightening contributions to the flourishing business culture of our time and we should honour him from the heart with this, his jubilee exhibition.

„Die Welt des Grafik-Design in der Galerie von Oertzen"
Städtische Galerie im Karmeliterkloster, Frankfurt/M.
vom 6. September – 5. Oktober 1997
Deutsches Plakatmuseum, Essen
vom 26. März – 3. Mai 1998

Die Galerie

Mit diesem Katalog stellt die
Galerie von Oertzen aus
ihrem Gesamtprogramm von
40 Ausstellungen 16 ausgewählte,
international renommierte
Grafik-Designer und
Design-Agenturen vor.

Kuratoren der Ausstellung:

Klaus Klemp,
Leiter der Abteilung Kultur
im Amt für Wissenschaft und Kunst
der Stadt Frankfurt am Main

Professor Olaf Leu,
Fachhochschule Mainz

Frieder Mellinghoff,
Deutsches Plakatmuseum, Essen

Klaus Klemp

1 | Design ausstellen

In Deutschland herrschen die Ingenieure. Ob im Inland oder Ausland, das alte Vorurteil hält sich hartnäckig, und manchmal, so scheint es zumindest, erhält es unerwartet neuen Auftrieb. Noch immer glauben viele, daß der deutsche Tüftelgeist auch die Zukunft meistern mag. Die althergebrachten Industriebereiche sind jedoch mächtig im Abstieg.
Die Produktion von Industrie- und Konsumgütern, so lesen wir es täglich in der Zeitung, sie verlagert sich mehr und mehr nach Osteuropa und nach Südostasien. Eine progressive Internationalisierung der Produktion ist durch einen immer größer werdenden Automatisierungsgrad bedingt. CNC-Maschinen ersetzen den qualifizierten Facharbeiter, und auf vielen Produktionsstraßen in Asien kontrolliert schon heute nicht mehr der Mensch, sondern der Computer den Herstellungsprozeß. Der Lohnkostenfaktor entscheidet über den Standort.

Neben der Technik beeinflußt daher mehr und mehr die Gestaltung die Wettbewerbsfähigkeit eines Produktes. Dabei ist es nicht immer eine eindimensionale Funktionsästhetik, die über den Absatz und über die Akzeptanz entscheidet. Die italienischen Möbel- und Interieurdesigner haben es in den achtziger Jahren vorgemacht: Ob etwas angenommen wird oder nicht, das hängt nicht nur mit der reibungslosen Gebrauchsfähigkeit zusammen, sondern hat auch eine starke emotionale Komponente. Gleiches gilt in besonderem Maße für das amerikanische Grafik-Design der sechziger Jahre.
Auch hier wurden die sogenannten funktionalen Regeln und Normen fast vollständig verlassen, ja zum Teil konterkariert. Der Ausbruch aus dem gestalterischen Maß der reinen Logik hat den Konsumenten und Lesern Spaß gemacht, und sie haben es mit einer entsprechenden Akzeptanz honoriert. Der Mensch, das vernunftbegabte Wesen, will eben nicht nur auf diese reduziert werden, die Ratio ist stets nur die eine Seite eines sehr viel komplexeren Menschseins. Einen großen Anteil

nehmen das Sentiment und die Subjektivität ein. Schon in der Hochphase der Zweiten Industriellen Revolution wußten die Produzenten und Designer um die Bedeutung des sinnlichen Eindrucks ihrer Produkte:

„Die Vorstellung, es genüge für den Ingenieur völlig, daß ein Bauwerk, ein Gerät, eine Maschine, die er schafft, einen Zweck erfülle, ist irrig; noch irriger ist der neuerdings oft gehörte Satz, daß, wenn sie einen Zweck erfülle, sie zugleich auch schön sei."

Hermann Muthesius, 1909

Seit gegen Ende des 17. Jahrhunderts Kunst und Technik getrennte Wege gingen, also seit der Ersten Industriellen Revolution der Dampfmaschine, der Schwerindustrie und der Massenfertigung von Gebrauchsgegenständen, der Industrialisierung des Buchdrucks und der Großauflagen von Zeitungen und Plakaten, seit dieser Zeit entstand das, was wir heute Design nennen. Es war ein langer und schmerzvoller, mal erfolgreicher, mal untauglicher Versuch, zu einer gestalterischen Form zu gelangen, die mit dem Zeitgeist und dem Zivilisationsstandard in Übereinstimmung stand.

Begleitet wurde dieser Entwicklungsprozeß des Design von der öffentlichen Zurschaustellung und der daraus resultierenden Debatte über die Produkte: sei es in den großen Weltausstellungen seit der Mitte des 19. Jahrhunderts, sei es durch die sich bildenden Gewerbevereine oder die entstehenden Museen für Gestaltung. Die Protagonisten der Moderne hatten dabei eine ganz besondere Affinität zum Medium Ausstellung. Die erste größere Tätigkeit des jungen Walter Gropius war die Organisation einer Ausstellung über den Industriebau im Auftrag des Deutschen Werkbundes. Im Jahr 1930 führte die Zeitschrift „Das Neue Frankfurt" – eine der wichtigsten Publikationen der Zwischenkriegszeit zur modernen Gestaltung – eine breite Debatte über das Thema Ausstellungen. Der Kunsthistoriker Franz Roh schrieb seinerzeit:

„Man muß die Ausstellungsmöglichkeiten auf alle Gebiete ausdehnen, ‚Kunst'-Ausstellungen selbstverständlich erweitern zu solchen optischer Gestaltungen überhaupt… Die fruchtbarste Zwischenstufe zwischen vollsinnlicher Anschauung und notwendiger Abstraktion gibt eben nicht das Lesebuch, sondern die Ausstellung."

Dieser hohe Stellenwert, den Gestaltungsausstellungen in der Weimarer Republik erreicht hatten, wurde nach 1945

lange Zeit nicht wiedererlangt. Dem Wirtschaftsboom der fünf-
ziger und sechziger Jahre erlag das kritische Interesse an einer
Auseinandersetzung mit unserer neuen zwei- und dreidimensionalen Umwelt weitgehend. Erst im Nachgang des gesell-
schaftlichen Umbruchs seit Mitte der sechziger Jahre erlangte
die Reflexion mit den Waren und Bildern unserer Gegenwart
ein neues Interesse. Bereits bestehende Einrichtungen wie das
Münchner Stadtmuseum oder neue wie das Deutsche Plakatmuseum in Essen begannen eine umfangreiche öffentliche
Auseinandersetzung über die visuellen Phänomene des Grafik-
Designs.

Das, was bislang zumeist nur von sekundärem Interesse
war, rückte nun in den Mittelpunkt: die visuelle Gestaltung
öffentlicher Räume, die Erscheinungsbilder und Werbebotschaf-
ten von großen Unternehmen und die staatlichen und kommu-
nalen Selbstdarstellungen und Bürgerkontakte. Damit einher
ging ein erweiterter internationaler Blick. Die wirtschaftlich
erstarkte Bundesrepublik überwand das Neo-Biedermeier der
Adenauer-Ära und öffnete sich zunehmend vor allem anglo-
amerikanischen Einflüssen. Zeitschriften wie die von Willy Fleckhaus gestaltete „twen" schufen ein neues Lebensgefühl. Was
zunächst vor allem für die Popmusik und die Jugendkultur galt,
gewann schon bald auch in der Werbung und im Corporate
Design der Unternehmen an Terrain.

Aber nicht nur die großen Ausstellungshäuser, die Printmedien und das Fernsehen veränderten die visuellen Para-
meter, sondern viele kleinere, vor allem private Initiativen tru-
gen erheblich dazu bei. Hier einzureihen ist die seit 1967
bestehende Tätigkeit der Galerie von Oertzen in Frankfurt am
Main, die sich seit 1984 konsequent dem internationalen
Grafik-Design verschrieben hat. Wer hinter dieser Galerie eine
kommerzielle Unternehmung vermutet, der irrt und hat doch
auch recht. Die von Oertzen GmbH ist ein ebenso traditions-
reiches wie technisch modernes Unternehmen des Druckvor-
stufenbereichs; die „Galerie von Oertzen" ist das ebenso
leidenschaftliche wie ideelle Kind Hans-Christoph von Oertzens,
das dem „Galeristen" nie auch nur eine Mark eingebracht hat.
In einer jahrelangen Allianz mit dem Frankfurter Designer und
Designvermittler Olaf Leu hat diese Firmengalerie in den
vergangenen zwölf Jahren ein Ausstellungsprogramm hervor-
gebracht, das vielen Design-Museen gut zu Gesicht stehen würde.

Die Galerie von Oertzen, das war und das ist die profunde
Adresse für alle Insider und Grafik-Design-Interessierten im
Rhein-Main-Gebiet und weit darüber hinaus. Die Vermittlungs-
arbeit zum Thema Designqualität, die hier in einem Dutzend von
Jahren erbracht wurde, ist das eine, die unzähligen Kontakte,
die bei den Vernissagen, Vorträgen und Symposien im Laufe der
Jahre entstanden sind, das andere. Nicht hoch genug zu schät-
zen sind solche Orte der Kommunikation, denn sie sind es, die
den Designprozeß weitertreiben, die den Transfer zwischen den
unterschiedlichen Positionen und Generationen ermöglichen.
Viele Galerien von Oertzen braucht das Land.

2 | Hans-Christoph von Oertzen
Die Galerie, Idee und Wirklichkeit

Die Beendigung des 2. Weltkrieges und damit auch der Aufhebung der Unterdrückung von Werken der sogenannten „entarteten Kunst" führte in Deutschland in weiten Bevölkerungskreisen zu einem erhöhten Kunstinteresse und damit verbundenen Aktivitäten. Die Öffnung einer Welt, die uns für viele Jahre verschlossen war, führte zu einem neuen, gesteigerten Lebensgefühl. Man wollte die Künstler kennenlernen und mit ihnen an diesem neuen Aufbruch teilhaben. Mein persönliches Interesse fand ich im Aufbau eines eigenen grafischen Betriebes.

So entstand in Wiesbaden, dorthin vor der sowjetischen Besatzungsmacht aus Ostdeutschland geflohen, ein neuer Freundeskreis, vorwiegend aus Malern, Bildhauern, Galeristen und Architekten. Auf Anregung der Wiesbadener Malerin, Kunstpädagogin und Galeristin Christa Moering kam es zur Gründung der Galerie von Oertzen; sie schlug vor, Künstler aus ihrem Umkreis auch einem Frankfurter Publikum vorzustellen.

Die Malerin
Christa Moering

Mein Gedanke bei der Gründung der Galerie richtete sich nicht darauf, einen weiteren Geschäftszweig meinem in Frankfurt ansässigen Unternehmen – Verlag und grafischer Betrieb – anzugliedern. Ich wollte nicht Kunsthändler sein. Die Galerie sollte in erster Linie den am künstlerischen Geschehen der Gegenwart Interessierten dienen, jedoch nicht nur für das von außen kommende Publikum, sondern auch für die im Betrieb tätigen Mitarbeiter, die täglich in die Kunst der Typografie und der grafischen Bildgestaltung eingebunden waren. Die Idee war, ein Begegnungs- und Kommunikationszentrum für alle diejenigen zu schaffen, für die die Kunst der Gegenwart ein vorrangiges Anliegen war. Dabei war mir natürlich auch die Imagepflege des Unternehmens wichtig. Die Kunst der Typografen und Lithografen sollte via Galerie einen verlängerten Arm erhalten.

Der Start erfolgte im Herbst 1967 mit dem Berliner, seit Ende des Krieges in Wiesbaden lebenden Maler Erwin Filter, es folgten Peter Schermuly, Günther Stiller, Hans Laabs und Christa Moering. Schnell erweiterte sich der Kreis durch eine freundschaftliche Verbindung mit dem in Ibiza ansässigen Anglo-Afrikaner Ivan Spence, der der Galerie Künstler von internationalem Rang zuführte.

Doch nach den ersten 12 Ausstellungen wurde mir klar, daß ich, ohne mich im Kunsthandel zu engagieren, die Galerie nicht zum Erfolg führen konnte. Die ausgestellten Künstler erwarteten Verkäufe, besonders die aus dem Ausland kommenden, zum Teil von weit her angereist. Das eigene Verlags- und Druckereiunternehmen verlangte auch mehr und mehr den vollen persönlichen Einsatz.

So entschied ich mich, für die Ausstellungsaktivitäten eine Pause einzulegen. Dies währte bis zum Jahr 1984.

Im Jahr 1983 wurde in unserem grafischen Betrieb der Bleisatz eingestellt, und die Verführung der hierdurch frei werdenden Räume war so groß, daß ich beschloß, die Galerie wieder ins Leben zu rufen. Inzwischen hatte sich die Firma von Oertzen als Druckvorstufenunternehmen mit einer größeren Anzahl von Werbeagenturen, Großunternehmen aus Industrie und Handel als Auftraggeber erfolgreich etabliert. So lag es nahe, diesem Publikum im Rahmen von Ausstellungen Beispiele des internationalen Top-Grafik-Designs zu präsentieren. In diese Zeit fiel der Beginn einer engeren Zusammenarbeit mit dem weit über die Region der Bundesrepublik bekannten und erfolgreichen Grafik-Designer Professor Olaf Leu.

Leu war über viele Jahre Chairman der deutschen Dependance des Type Directors Club of New York und auch als Juror für dessen jährliche Wettbewerbe tätig. So war er ein hervorragender Kenner der Szene des internationalen Top-Designs. Die herausragende Stellung der Galerie von Oertzen als Repräsentant des internationalen high-rank Designs verdankt die Galerie überwiegend den Verbindungen, die Olaf Leu für sie schuf.

Die persönlichen Kontakte zu Künstlern aus vier Kontinenten – Europa, Nah- und Fernost, Nord- und Südamerika und Australien – bildeten für die Mitarbeiter unseres Unternehmens und natürlich auch für die Gäste, hier besonders die Studenten der umliegenden Hochschulen, eine große Bereicherung.

So gelang es, für die Galerie Professoren der Hochschule für Gestaltung in Offenbach am Main, der Fachhochschulen in Darmstadt, Mainz, Wiesbaden und Mannheim dafür zu engagieren, ihre Studenten anzuregen, an den jeweils am Tage nach der Vernissage unter Anwesenheit der Künstler veranstalteten Workshops teilzunehmen. So hat sich manche persönliche Freundschaft zwischen den Künstlern, ihren Freunden und dem Galeristen gebildet.

Leider ist es im Rahmen der Präsentation im Karmeliterkloster nur möglich, einen Teil der 40 Ausstellungen, die die Galerie in den vergangenen Jahren dem Publikum darbot, vorzustellen. Ganz verzichten muß ich auf den ersten Teil meiner Ausstellungsperiode von 1967–1969 und auf die Ausstellung der Grafik von Max Slevogt aus Privatbesitz im Jahr 1975.

Im Rahmen dieser ersten Ausstellungsphase wurden in 12 Ausstellungen die nachfolgenden Malerinnen und Maler vorgestellt:

Erwin Filter, Deutschland
Peter Schermuly, Deutschland
Hans Laabs, Deutschland
Günther Stiller, Deutschland
Alberto Gutiérrez, Columbien
Bernhard C. Eder, Österreich
Christa Moering, Deutschland
Eduardo Urculo, Spanien
Natale Sapone, Italien
Shiro Sasaki, Japan
Becky Sandstede, Deutschland
Gisela Aulfes-Daeschler, Deutschland

Auch von der zweiten Ausstellungsphase von 1984–1995, die bis auf wenige Ausnahmen Künstler und Studios des internationalen Grafik-Designs umfaßte, kann ich nur 14 von insgesamt 28 Ausstellungen zeigen. Es sind:

Anton Stankowski, Deutschland
Oswaldo Miranda, Brasilien
Olaf Leu, Deutschland
Zdenek Ziegler, Tschechien
Takenobu Igarashi, Japan
Jean Widmer, Frankreich
Gottschalk & Ash Int'l, Schweiz, Kanada
Total Design, Holland

Joe Duffy, The Duffy Design Group, USA
Three Australians:
    Ken Cato
    Garry Emery
    Barrie Tucker
Susumu Endo, Japan
Josse Goffin, Belgien
The Partners, England
Yves Zimmermann, Spanien

Leider nicht zeigen kann ich die Arbeiten von:

Friedrich Poppl, Deutschland
Mike Rose, Deutschland
Papier-Ideen, Akademie der bildenden Künste,
    Stuttgart, Deutschland
Henrik Strömberg, Finnland
Reiner Seibold, Deutschland
Zlatko Prica, Kroatien
Manfred Kage, Deutschland
Dietrich Ebert, Deutschland
Asher Kalderon, Israel
12 Brasilianer, Brasilien
Wort-Bild-Wort, TDC New York, USA
Jan Mlodozeniec, Polen
Martin Solomon, USA
Circulo de Creativos Argentinos, Argentinien

Doch bin ich der Überzeugung, daß diese Auswahl Ihnen ein
gutes Bild über das Engagement der Galerie vermitteln wird.

Olaf Leu

3 Grafik-Design als Ausstellungsobjekt.
Die Geschichte der „grafischen"
Galerien in Deutschland.

Vorspiel:

Im Jahr 1960 wurde in New York, hauptsächlich auf
Initiative von Aaron Burns, das ICTA – The International Center
for the Typographic Arts – gegründet. Die Idee dieser Institution war der weltweite Austausch von Fachwissen, gestalterischen Ideen, kritischen Stellungnahmen, Besprechung
richtungweisender Entwurfsarbeiten, Veröffentlichungen und
Ausstellungen.

Organisatorischer und zentraler Anlaufpunkt war New
York, das gerade in diesen sechziger Jahren auf dem Höhe-
punkt kreativen Wirkens war. Erst Jahrzehnte später sollte man
das, was damals auf dem Gebiet des amerikanischen Grafik-
Designs passierte, als das Wirken „der Neuen Amerikanischen
Schule" bezeichnen.

Das ICTA – so die Kurzform – basierte einerseits auf
der straff geführten Zentrale in New York, andererseits auf sogenannten Ländersektionen und Einzelmitgliedschaften.

Das ICTA und dessen Mitgliedschaft eröffnete nicht nur
weltweite briefliche und auch persönliche Kontakte wie
Besuchsprogramme oder Besucherbetreuung durch Gleichge-
sinnte, es war auch die Kontaktstelle zu bestehenden anderen
grafischen Organisationen wie z. B. zum Art Directors Club
oder zum Type Directors Club of New York, zum AIGA, zur STD,
zu Kollegenorganisationen in Kanada, Japan, England und
Holland.

Aus diesem Netzwerk entwickelten sich im Lauf der Jahre
Aktivitäten, die auf der einen Seite des Atlantiks organisiert –
man denke dabei an die beiden großen Weltausstellungen der
typografischen Künste „Typomundus 1 und 2" – und auf der
anderen Seite von den einzelnen Ländersektionen eigenverant-
wortlich gestaltet wurden.

Der damaligen Existenz einer so weltweit agierenden Organisation wie die des ICTA verdanken die Galerien in Deutschland ihr Ausstellungsprogramm und damit überhaupt ihr Zustandekommen.

Hauptspiel:

Im Herbst 1964 wurde ich anläßlich meines ersten Besuches in den USA, dabei durchaus bewußt auf den Spuren einer ICTA-Mitgliedschaft wandelnd, mit dem Aufbau einer ICTA-Sektion Deutschland betraut. Wir hatten damals schon mehrere deutsche Einzelmitgliedschaften, besaßen aber keine eigene nationale Sektion. Diese zu organisieren war meine Aufgabe als neuernannter Sekretär, der damals unter den präsidialen Fittichen von Kurt Weidemann agierte. Die Mitgliedschaft der neuen Sektion war damals über die ganze Republik verstreut, so daß persönliche Treffen nur vereinzelt möglich waren. Eine andere Aktivität, die eine viel größere Wirkung entfalten sollte, war die Installierung von Ausstellungen, die via ICTA-Netzwerk zur Verfügung gestellt werden konnten.

Aber wo waren dafür die Ausstellungsplätze?

Damals in diesen Anfangssechzigern war ich für die Eigenwerbung der Firma Typo Knauer in Frankfurt am Main tätig. Bei meinem hier vorerwähnten ersten USA-Besuch lernte ich insbesondere in New York die in Layoutsetzereien installierten Galerien kennen. Diese hatten die Aufgabe, stets das Neueste auf dem Gebiet des Grafik-Designs aufzuzeigen und dazu so etwas zu pflegen und auszubauen, was man heute als Kundenkontakte, Kundenpflege und Kundenbindung bezeichnet. Es war meist der Vorraum, das Vestibül, das geschickt mit der Multifunktion eines Empfangs und einer Galerie kombiniert wurde. Die erste dieser speziell nur für Grafik-Design eingerichteten Galerien war die in New York ansässige „The little Composing Room", gegründet schon im Jahr 1921. Sie wurde von Dr. Robert Leslie, dem Inhaber von Photolettering, betrieben. Diese Galerie-Idee nahm ich mit nach Frankfurt am Main zu Heinz Knauer, der daraufhin seinen großzügig bemessenen Vorraum ebenfalls mit der Doppelfunktion eines Empfangs und einer Galerie ausstattete.

Im Frühjahr 1965 wurde die erste Galerie für Grafik-Design in Deutschland, die Knauer Expo in der Schleusenstraße, unmittelbar am Frankfurter Hauptbahnhof gelegen, mit der

Präsentation des grafischen Œuvres des Amerikaners Herb
Lubalin eröffnet. Das ehrgeizige Programm von vier Ausstellungen im Jahr ließ sich nur in den ersten drei Jahren durch-
halten, wie die gesamte Galerie-Idee ebenfalls nur bis zur
ersten wirtschaftlichen Rezession in den Anfangssiebzigern
aufrechterhalten werden konnte. Auch durch mein vorheriges
Ausscheiden aus der Ausstellungsleitung und einer ungenü-
genden Nachfolge sowie dem Erlöschen des ICTA waren
sämtliche Beweggründe einer grafischen Galerietätigkeit ent-
zogen.

Ein halbes Jahr später, im Oktober 1965, eröffnete die
Bauersche Gießerei in der Hamburger Allee 45 ihre „galerie bg"
mit der Präsentation der 11. Type Directors Show of New York –
auch diese Ausstellung war durch Vermittlung des ICTA-Aus-
stellungsnetzes zustande gekommen.

Frankfurt am Main hatte nun zwei grafische Galerien –
aber beiden, Knauer Expo und „galerie bg", waren nur wenige
Jahre des Wirkens beschieden.

Die Idee einer Galerie für Grafik-Design setzte sich
in München im Frühjahr 1966 als zweite Station in Deutschland
unter dem Begriff „Intergraphis" im BMW-Pavillon am Lenbachplatz fort. Die erste Präsentation war hier das Corporate
Design des Columbia Broadcasting System – kurz CBS genannt
– unter Lou Dorfsman. Auch dieser großzügig angelegten
Galerie waren nur wenige aktive Ausstellungsjahre beschieden.

Im gleichen Jahr, Herbst 1966, entstand in Stuttgart
der Ableger der Knauer Expo in Frankfurt am Main, ebenfalls
eine Vestibül-Galerie, die das Ausstellungsprogramm ihrer
Frankfurter Mutter an das Stuttgarter Publikum weiterreichte.

1967 war das Gründungsjahr der dritten Frankfurter Galerie, der Galerie von Oertzen, die allerdings nicht das Grafik-
Design, sondern die freie Kunst zum Ausstellungsobjekt erhob.
Insofern darf man hier den kleinen Unterschied zu den anderen
beiden Frankfurter Galerien sehen.

Die Galerie von Oertzen verzeichnet auch so zwei
Ausstellungsepochen, die von 1967 bis 1969 mit freier Kunst,
und von 1984 bis heute mit Grafik-Design.

Die ersten Jahre der Siebziger sind gleichbedeutend mit
dem Erlöschen aller Ausstellungsaktivitäten in der gesamten,
damals noch geteilten Republik. Erst mit Beginn der achtziger
Jahre zeigt sich noch einmal ein Aufflammen der alten Idee

der Mittsechziger. Einmal ist es die Tätigkeit des Studios für Typographie und Reprosatz, Schumacher-Gebler in München, das für einige Folgejahre so etwas zustande brachte, was man als eine konsequente Ausstellungstätigkeit bezeichnen konnte – ohne sich als ausgesprochene Galerie zu bezeichnen –, und auf der anderen Seite ist es im Jahr 1984 die Wiederaufnahme der Galerietätigkeit der Ausstellungsinstitution von Oertzen.Der Stadt Frankfurt am Main sollte so bis zuletzt die einzige Galerie für Grafik-Design erhalten bleiben.

Nachspiel:

Mit Ausnahme der „Intergraphis" in München waren es Unternehmen des Pre-Press-Bereiches, die sich der Galerietätigkeit verschrieben hatten. Auf private Initiative gegründet, waren sie natürlich auch von den wirtschaftlichen Schwingungen abhängig; insofern nimmt es nicht wunder, wenn man heute darüber in der Vergangenheitsform spricht. Bis auf die Ausnahme der noch gegenwärtigen Galerie von Oertzen. Interessant im nachhinein ist die Tatsache, daß sich alle Erstpräsentationen auf amerikanisches Material erstreckten, so im Fall beider Knauer Expos, Intergraphis und galerie bg. Die „Neue Amerikanische Schule" hatte so ihren Weg nach Deutschland gefunden und nachdrücklich das deutsche Grafik-Design mitgestaltet.

Friedrich Friedl

4 Zur Sache

Die Entwicklung der grafischen Gestaltung hat in unserem Jahrhundert eine enorme Entwicklung in Quantität und Qualität genommen. Gleichzeitig gab es tiefgreifende Wandlungen des gestalterischen Berufsbildes: der Weg von der Plakatmalerei zur Gebrauchsgrafik, dann zum Graphic Design und schließlich zur visuellen Kommunikation war begleitet, und meist sogar ausgelöst, von grundlegenden technischen Veränderungen, von Verfeinerungen des Formsuchens, von einer Erweiterung des konzeptionellen Überlegens.

Die Tatsache, daß die grafische Wirklichkeit in den Metropolen immer wieder Relikte vergangener Gestaltungs-phasen aufleben läßt, kann für den einen Betrachter Labsal und für den anderen Ärgernis sein, kann als Reichhaltigkeit oder als Regression bezeichnet werden, kann als Suche nach Alternative oder als Unvermögen eingeschätzt werden. Klarheit über die Bedeutung der reichhaltigen Erscheinungs-formen der Gestaltung und ihre objektive oder persönliche Einschätzung erfordert keinen genialistischen Instinkt oder naturbelassene Beharrung, sondern intensive Auseinander-setzung mit praktischen und theoretischen Ergebnissen.

Eine nüchterne Bestandsaufnahme zeigt, daß wir, trotz der wundervollen gestalterischen Entwicklungen, am Ende unseres Jahrhunderts (das auch ein Ende eines Jahrtausends ist) mit den gleichen Problemen konfrontiert sind wie am Anfang; die Sehnsucht nach privaten Mythologien und rührende Hoffnungsromantik bestimmten den Jugendstil und bestimmen die Gegenwart. Die Rebellion, die forsch den angewandten Gestalter als autonomen Künstler und eigenen Auftraggeber fordert, gehört zum gegenwärtigen intellektuellen Durch-einander und ist mehr eine selbstüberschätzende Angeberei, die bekannte avantgardistische Kunstpositionen in Dienst nimmt, als eine ernstzunehmende Position in der Kommuni-kationsgestaltung. Die immer konventioneller werdende unkonventionelle Haltung in der Gestaltung und die Sehnsucht nach der freien angewandten Gestaltung ersetzt nicht die Notwendigkeit seriöser visueller Kommunikation.

Die Kenntnisse, die zu diesem nach wie vor wichtigsten Ziel in der angewandten Gestaltung führen, werden durch eine immer oberflächlichere Rezeption der Lehre an den Hochschulen, durch den schneller werdenden Verschleiß der visuellen Zeichen, durch halbreligiöse Anbetungsprozesse und sonstigen Gestaltungstourismus immer seltener auf einem bemerkenswerten, weiterführenden Niveau erreicht.
Für die Kulturindustrie ist das kein Hinderungsgrund, ständig neue Gestaltungsstars in die Konsummanege zu werfen, mit dem Hinweis auf die neuen Formen, die aber meist keine neue Formen sind, mit dem Verlegen von Büchern, in denen nichts Intelligentes steht; mit dazu veranstalteten Ausstellungen, die diese Nichtigkeiten objektivieren. Dies alles ist zu registrieren, und nicht zu beklagen, denn wahrscheinlich war es nie anders. Das Benennen dieser Umstände sollte Anlaß sein, vielfältig nach aktiven Verbesserungen und Veränderungen zu suchen: mit theoretischen und praktischen Vorgehensweisen und Ergebnissen.

Die Kenntnisse über die Erscheinungsformen der grafischen Gestaltung bilden sich bei Nicht-Profis empirisch durch zufällig registrierte Ergebnisse heraus: Hier fällt ein Handzettel auf, dort ein Plakat, eine Plastiktüte, ein Fernsehspot. Dazu kommen Ausstellungen im kulturellen Bereich, die meist in Kunstgewerbemuseen stattfinden, die historische Entwicklungen aufzeigen und Gegenwart dort ahnen, wo nachempfundener Futurismus auf Büttenpapier wabert: verkunstete Privatismen ohne jegliche Relevanz oder professionellen Bezug. In manchen Regionen sind Fachmuseen anzutreffen, das Rhein-Main-Gebiet hat international attraktive Institutionen wie das Gutenberg-Museum in Mainz und das Klingspor-Museum in Offenbach, in denen ganze Handwerks- und Gestaltungsentwicklungen nachzuvollziehen sind. Immer wieder gab es private Versuche, das Interesse für bzw. das Geschäft mit Graphic Design zu aktivieren. Posterläden und Antiquariatsabteilungen nahmen sich dieser Möglichkeit an, selten mit Erfolg, selten mit Kenntnissen oder Bezügen zu den Berufen des Gestaltens.

Durch die wachsende Wertschätzung gestalteten Graphic Designs entstanden neue Foren für eine kontinuierliche Auseinandersetzung auf professionellem Niveau. Eine der bemerkenswertesten europäischen Galerien für Graphic Design, die international Maßstäbe gesetzt hat, ist seit 1972 die Print Gallery von Pieter Brattinga in Amsterdam. Hier wurden im Laufe der Jahre Ausstellungen von Projekten der einflußreichsten Graphic Designer veranstaltet, die Brattinga mit sicherem Blick für Qualität oft vor deren Berühmtwerden entdeckte. Die Galerie war als Ergänzung seiner Graphic Design-Agentur konzipiert.

Mit einem anderen Konzept erreichte seit 1984 die Galerie von Oertzen in Frankfurt gleiche Wichtigkeit und Ausstrahlung. In den Räumen des fachlich überregional erfolgreichen Full-Service-Unternehmens für Text-Bild-Kommunikations-Medien untergebracht, zeigt die Galerie eine interessante Symbiose von klassischem und neuem Handwerk, mit dem kulturellen Anspruch, die besten internationalen grafischen Ergebnisse nicht nur zu zeigen, sondern auch erleben zu lassen.

Diese Kulturereignisse im grafischen Bereich, die jeweils ein Zusammenspiel von hervorragenden Ausstellungen, von ausgesuchten Eröffnungsreden, von den Kontaktmöglichkeiten zu den vorgestellten Gestaltern, dem anwesenden Fachpublikum und zu den Firmenmitarbeitern waren, sind im Rhein-Main-Gebiet von einem vielfältig interessierten Publikum äußerst positiv und aktiv rezipiert worden. Die am Tag nach den Ausstellungseröffnungen veranstalteten Workshops unter Mitwirkung der jeweiligen Gestalter glichen Gastvorlesungen an Hochschulen, die auch vor allem für Studierende der visuellen Kommunikation aus Darmstadt, Mainz, Offenbach, Wiesbaden und Mannheim eine intensive Einblicknahme und Auseinandersetzung mit dem Werk und dem Gestalter ermöglichten.

Wenn man überlegt, daß die besten Gestalter aus Brasilien, Japan, Frankreich, Polen, England oder Deutschland eingeladen und ausgestellt wurden, kann man nachempfinden, welche Kontinuität an Qualität hier zu erleben war, welche Einwirkung dieser Aktivitäten auf die professionelle gestalterische Szene der Region und darüber hinaus hatte.
Die Galerie von Oertzen hat sich um die Vermittlung professioneller Qualität in der gestalterischen Kunst verdient gemacht.

Frieder Mellinghoff

 Background

Der Unternehmer Hans-Christoph von Oertzen hat vorzugsweise ein Arbeitskonzept vertreten, das sich aus mehreren Ebenen zusammenfügte. Grundsätzlich war sein komplexes Denken dem wirtschaftlichen Agieren gemäß. Aber welche Ebenen er einzog, um sein Unternehmen erfolgreich zu entwickeln, hatte durchaus persönliche Gründe: Nach dem zweiten Weltkrieg gehörte es zu seinen privaten Anliegen, sich mit bildender Kunst zu beschäftigen, künstlerische Produktionen anderer Menschen vor Augen zu führen und dies auch zum Anlaß von Geselligkeit zu machen.

Die Kunst findet man in der Begegnung mit den Werken, mit ihren Autoren, aber auch mit Freunden, die aus Farben und Formen viele Wahrnehmungen ablesen und eine Fülle von Erkenntnissen beziehen. Das Besondere liegt darin, daß in solchen Kreisen mit einander vertrauter Menschen beglückende Übereinstimmungen zutage treten oder aber Toleranz gefragt ist, da sich das eigene Ego von anderen differenziert. Geselligkeit war also nicht Selbstzweck, sondern eher eine diskrete Schule des Umgangs miteinander, was sich im Alltag auf Unternehmenskultur übertragen ließ. – Darüber hinaus hat gewiß die beispielhafte Initialkraft von Künstlern und ihre ästhetische Bildung eine Faszination auf diese Generation ausgestrahlt, die sich dem Mut, der Kraft und der existentiellen Risikobereitschaft nahefühlten. Dies alles konnte sicher der Wiesbadener Freundeskreis für sich in Anspruch nehmen, dem Hans-Christoph von Oertzen angehörte.

Dieser philanthropisch-idealistische Ansatz wurde nach wenigen Jahren mit zwei Entwicklungstendenzen konfrontiert, die zu Entscheidungen führen mußten: Der sich ausweitende kaufmännische Umgang mit Kunstwerken im Galeriebetrieb unserer Großstädte erzeugte Druck von außen, und das wachsende Unternehmen, das der Print-Kommunikation diente, erforderte von innen her eine Konzentration auf geschäftliche

Aufgaben. Schließlich kam – nach einigen Jahren der Unter-
brechung aller Ausstellungsaktivitäten – die Synthese aus den
USA, vermittelt durch Olaf Leu. Letzterer hatte jenseits des
Atlantik beobachtet, wie geschickt inszenierend moderne Satz-
studios mit der Materie des Graphik-Design umgingen, wie
sie die ästhetischen Komponenten der Auftragsarbeit als eine
qualitative Zugabe in kleineren innerbetrieblichen Ausstellungen thematisierten und unbezahlbare Leistungspotentiale zur
Schau stellten.

Dies war genau das, was in die Tätigkeitsmerkmale des
Unternehmens von Oertzen hineinpaßte und obendrein eine
Fülle von geschäftsnahen Aspekten absetzte. Präsentationen
von herausragender typographischer und ikonographischer
Gestaltung mit dem Ziel der Informations- und Wertvermitt-
lung in einer wiederbelebten Galerie von Oertzen entsprechen
den selbstgesteckten Zielen des Hausherrn. Sie beziehen alle
Mitarbeiter in die Betrachtung darüber ein, was zeitgemäße
graphische Ausdrucksformen sein können. Sie weisen über den
berüchtigten Tellerrand hinaus. Sie geben Anlaß, Freude und
Bewunderung wiederum in geselliger Form mit Freunden des
Hauses, Auftraggebern und Neugierigen zu teilen. Sie vermitteln ein Gefühl dafür, was man von der Zukunft an kreativen
Vorstößen erwarten kann, und damit eröffnen sie Neuland.

Ein besonderes Verdienst des Hausherrn liegt in seiner
Gastgeberrolle. Er lädt die Gestalter der ausgestellten Arbeiten
zu einer lebendigen Zeugenschaft ein. Oft erhält eine speziell
für die Galerie von Oertzen vom Künstler entwickelte Arbeit
als „work in process" in der Galerie den letzten Schliff auf einer
Druckmaschine. Und schließlich führt er sie mit jungen Menschen zusammen, die in der Ausbildung stehen und versuchen
wollen, in die Fußstapfen der großen Meister zu treten.
Daß solch eine anregende Quelle der Anschauung und Erfahrung zum heißen Tip in der regionalen Szene wird, versteht
sich von selbst. Damit ist also auch ein werblicher Unterneh-
menszweck erfüllt, der den Auftraggebern ebenso nahegeht
wie strebsamen zukünftigen Mitarbeitern.

Die Auswahl seiner Werkdarstellungen ist international
und gezielt: Anton Stankowski, zum Beispiel, ist ein künst-
lerischer Gestalter, der seine ästhetische Regeneration
über Jahrzehnte in der Gratwanderung zwischen bildender
Kunst und funktionaler Gebrauchsgraphik fand. Wie ein

Bauhäusler baute er Brücken zwischen beiden Disziplinen und demonstrierte, wie der Künstler in seinen Bildern das Absolute einer Form erarbeitet und wie der Designer dieses visuelle Ergebnis in der Alltagskommunikation verwendbar macht. Die Ökonomie der Mittel war stets ein wichtiger Aspekt dabei. Beide Stränge hat er wie ein belastbares Zugseil für die Wirtschaft miteinander verbunden und hierin dem Verlangen von Hans-Christoph von Oertzen entsprochen. Stankowskis Markenzeichen und Erscheinungsbilder sind für jedermann inzwischen selbstverständliche optische Akzente geworden. Die Ausstellung im Unternehmen öffnete jedoch einen viel breiteren Fächer und zeigte, aus welch reichhaltiger, ästhetisch-experimenteller Erfahrung der Gestalter seine Konsequenzen zog.

Buchstäblich aus einer anderen Welt stammten die Arbeiten von Takenobu Igarashi, der sich bereits seit Jahren des CAD bediente und daraus am liebsten typographische Bilder entwickelte. Ihre Basis war natürlich überwiegend das Alphabet des „western style", doch baute er dreidimensionale Formen daraus, die dem gegenständlichen Ursprung chinesisch/japanischer Zeichenschrift nahekommen. Gleichzeitig verweist er mit diesem formalen Konzept auf das Verhältnis vom Wort zum Raum, auf die Tatsache, daß jede Botschaft Raum durchqueren muß und daß seine dreidimensionalen Wortbilder bereits als Volumen im Raum erscheinen.

Von kulturgeschichtlicher Bedeutung waren die ausgestellten Zahlentafeln der verschiedenen Jahrgänge des MOMA-Kalenders, eines Projekts, das zunächst auf fünf Jahre mit dem Museum of Modern Art in New York vereinbart war, später auf zehn Jahre erweitert wurde. Es hatte einen Wettstreit zwischen Mensch und Maschine, Grafiker und Computer zum Ziel. Zehn Jahre lang zwölf Monatsblätter mit Tageszahlen, die nicht einmal einen Zwilling haben durften (wie gnädig ist doch die Natur ...). Diese intellektuellen und experimentellen Dimensionen des Graphik-Design und speziell der Typographie zu betrachten, war eine Lehre für alle, die hinschauen und hinhören durften!

Während andere Unternehmen derartige Ausstellungstätigkeiten nach einiger Zeit wieder aufgegeben haben, waren für Hans-Christoph von Oertzen die Prinzipien seiner Galerie-Idee so bedeutsam und das positive Echo auf seine Mühen damit so rundherum befriedigend, daß er den verbreiteten Ermüdungserscheinungen nicht erlag. Er hat – abgestimmt mit Olaf Leu – in seinen Betrieb ein Testfeld integriert, das gerade in unseren Jahren der kommunikationstechnischen Neuerungen auf breiter Front eine spannende Schnittstelle bildet zwischen Tradition und Innovation.

Zweifellos ist es ein „Kunststück", solche Aktivitäten nicht zur betriebswirtschaftlichen Belastung werden zu lassen. Es wäre aber ein Jammer, wenn man die zu sammelnden Erfahrungen nur in abstracto der akademischen Theoriebildung überließe.

Insofern hat Hans-Christoph von Oertzen in sein Konzeptionsgebäude noch eine neue Ebene von gesellschaftlicher Bedeutung eingezogen. Wir sollten genau hinschauen, was sich darauf abspielt, wir sollten ihm für seine vorbildlichen Beiträge zur ausstrahlenden Unternehmenskultur danken, und wir sollten ihn mit dieser Jubiläumsausstellung herzlich feiern!

Born in Gelsenkirchen on the 18th July 1906, Anton Stankowski studied under Max Burchartz at the Folkwangschule in Essen from *1927-1929*, when he was summoned to work as photographer and typographer in the renowned "Advertising-Studio" of Max Dalang, which is where he developed "constructive graphics". Since *1951* he has had his own studio in Stuttgart. In *1959* he introduced the slant element into constructive painting, in *1976* he was appointed as professor by Baden-Württemberg and in *1982* he was guest of honour at the Villa Massimo in Rome. In *1983* Anton Stankowski founded the non-profit making "Stankowski Stiftung" for the promotion of "Art and Design" and in *1985* he made a large donation of paintings, graphic designs and drawings to the Kunsthaus Zürich, the Staatsgalerie Stuttgart and to the art collection of Gelsenkirchen. He has been actively promoting exhibitions both at home and abroad since *1928*, and his designs for company logos and corporate identities have shaped the images of the great multinational corporations of today.

> ...to find, to simplify, to bring to reality and
> to humanise, those are the motivating factors
> in my work. In this respect, it is the last,
> the humanising, that is the most difficult...

quotation for an opening
speech by Günther Wirth

Exhibition contribution

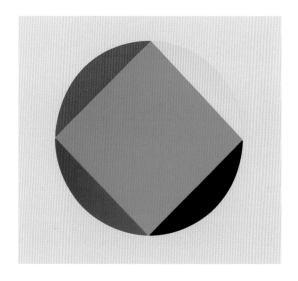

Oswaldo Miranda (Miran), art director, cartoonist, poster designer and publisher of Grafica Magazine, is a founder member of the Clube dos Direcyores de Arte no Brasil and a member of the Type Directors Club of New York, the Art Directors Club of New York, and the Alliance Graphique Internationale.

Miranda has been awarded more than 450 prizes for his graphic art, of which 75% are international ones. Among the prizes he received in Brazil were 25 gold and 35 silver medals, awarded by the Clube de Criacao de São Paulo.

Recently, in 1995, Miranda was awarded the Distinctive Merit Awards at the 74th annual show of the Art Directors Club of New York. In the same year he received 4 awards at the International Show of the TDC-Type Directors Club. In the years 1991, 1993 and 1994 he was awarded the Certificate of Merit and Excellence in the CA-Communication Arts Annual and also the best in Graphic Design annual 1997 and Three Merit Certificate in Brno-Biennial, Czech Republic. Contributing to his high reputation as a graphic designer and cartoonist are his many publications in the international technical press and the many exhibitions arranged by him.

...Oswaldo Miranda combines within himself several talents: the playful organist on the typographic organ, pulling out all the stops at the same time; the passionate illustrator, and the possessed calligrapher. All these gifts are held together by the administrative and organizational flair of the born art director...

quotation from an article by
Olaf Leu

Piet Zwart.

Visões de Utopias

De Stijl.

O homem faz parte da natureza. O que faz parte da natureza do homem é o estilo.

DE STIJL'S WORK 1917 1931

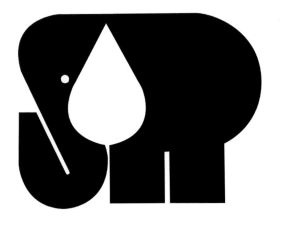

Olaf Leu Design & Partner

Olaf Leu was born in Chemnitz in 1936 and grew up in Biberach an der Riss. After eight years at school, he followed a three-year apprenticeship in typesetting from 1951-54, when he became a typographic designer at the art studio of the Bauersche Giesserei. Then in 1957 and 1958 he was assistant to the creative directors in the Hanns W. Brose Advertising Agency in Frankfurt a. M. before working independently as a graphic designer and art director from 1959-70. In 1971 he founded Studios Olaf Leu Design in Frankfurt a. M., which in 1976 became Olaf Leu Design & Partner and continued to operate until 1991. After the sale of the Studio in 1991, Olaf Leu concentrated on writing for periodicals and on teaching, lecturing, holding seminars and doing jury-work in Europe, South and North America, India, Australia and New Zealand. He has taken part in many group exhibitions and in 60 one-man exhibitions. Olaf Leu has received over 310 awards in national and international graphic design. He is a life member of the Art Directors Club and the Type Directors Club of New York and was a co-founder of the graphic galleries movement in Germany. Since 1986 he has taught Corporate Design at the Fachhochschule in Mainz.

> ...Olaf Leu was one of the first to get involved in this international trend. His advertisements, calendars and cigarette packets became known all over the world. They all had an opulent form, which combined an Art Nouveau type elegance with the severity of functionalism but without the kitschy side of either being allowed to meet...

quotation by Friedrich Friedl

GROSS

MACHT

GROSS

MÄRZ MARCH MARS MARZO   APRIL APRIL AVRIL ABRIL

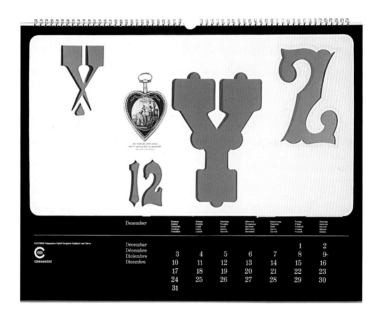

	Dezember	Sonntag Sunday Dimanche Domingo Domenica	Montag Monday Lundi Lunes Lunedi	Dienstag Tuesday Mardi Martes Martedi	Mittwoch Wednesday Mercredi Miércoles Mercoledi	Donnerstag Thursday Jeudi Jueves Giovedi	Freitag Friday Vendredi Viernes Venerdi	Samstag Saturday Samedi Sábado Sabato
	December						1	2
	Décembre	3	4	5	6	7	8	9
	Diciembre	10	11	12	13	14	15	16
	Dicembre	17	18	19	20	21	22	23
		24	25	26	27	28	29	30
		31						

61

Born in Prague on 27th October 1932, Zdenek Ziegler studied in Prague at the Technische Hochschule from *1955-1961*. Since *1990* he has taught at the Akademie für Kunst, Architektur und Design and he is a member of the Association Graphique Internationale. He has always been deeply involved in book and poster design, advertising graphics, exhibitions installation and (even under the communist regime) private work in graphics, as the list of his prizes and awards suggests: *1964* Award at the Typomundus, *1964* Award at the Internationale Plakatausstellung in Karlsbad, *1965* Silver medal at the International Exhibition in Colombo, Prize In the "Das schönste Buch des Jahres" competition (*1969, 1970, 1987, 1991, 1992, 1993, 1994, 1995, 1996*), *1978* Golden Hugo Prize in Chicago (for his film posters), *1979* Award at the Hollywood Report exhibition, *1982* Silver Plaque in Chicago, *1983* Bronze Hugo Prize in Chicago, *1987-1988* Award for the "Die besten Plakate des Jahres" competition.

> ...this exhibition, "Typo &", shows a sharp eye, a lively intellect and in places a subtle wit. But it also shows a sure feel for creative stimuli – wherever they may come from. To a remarkable extent, "Typo &" has worked out and formulated such stimuli in a new way, converting them into an internationally recognizable design, into an internationally valid language of form...

quotation from an opening speech
by Olaf Leu

Exhibition contribution

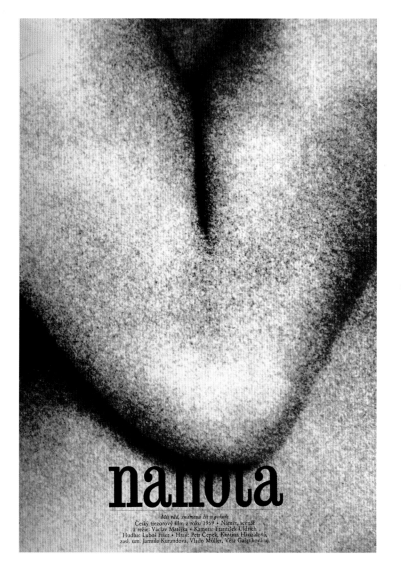

nahota

Mít rád, znamená žít v pokuře
Český trezorový film z roku 1969 • Námět, scénář
a režie: Václav Matějka • Kamera: František Uldrich
Hudba: Luboš Fišer • Hrají: Petr Čepek, Kristina Hanzalová,
zasl. um. Jarmila Kurandová, Vlado Müller, Věra Galatíková aj.

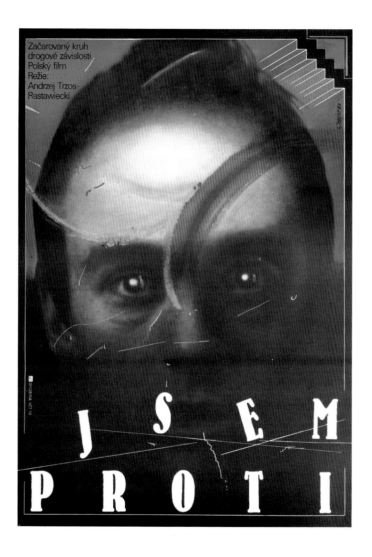

Začarovaný kruh
drogové závislosti
Polský film
Režie:
Andrzej Trzos-
Rastawiecki

VÝSTŘ E L
DO ZAD

Sovětský kriminální film
vzrušující pátrání
po vrahovi
úspěšného spisovatele

Hrají:
Lev Prygunov
Michail Volkov
Igor Ochlupin aj.

Režie:
Vladimir
Čebotarev

Takenobu Igarashi

Born in 1944 in Takikawa on Hokkaido, Takenobu Igarashi went to Tokyo in 1957. In 1961 he became a pupil of Prof. Masato Takahashi, graduating at the Tama University of Fine Arts. In 1968 he went to the University of California, where he took his Master's Degree in 1969. He returned to Tokyo in 1970 and established his own design office. From 1976-1979 he was a lecturer in the Design Department at UCLA and from 1979-1983 an instructor in the Department of Technology at Chiba University. Takenobu Igarashi is a designer and sculptor of international renown. He is known for a series of axonometric posters using alphabets and letterforms as well as shopping bags and calendars for The Museum of Modern Art, New York (MoMA); corporate identity projects for Suntory Limited; "Hibiki" sculpture for the entrance way of Suntory Hall in Tokyo; 150 limited edition sculptures for the Nissan "Infinity" showrooms in the United States and product design such as the Legame cordless telephone. His work is in the Permanent Collections of the Museum of Modern Art, New York, as well as other museums and universities throughout the world.

> ...through his three-dimensional letter projections and their further development into sculptures, he has turned the alphabet into an aesthetic object which transcends the purely communicative function of information transfer and invades the concrete world. In doing all this, he has expanded the mediating role of alphanumeric signs, he has broken through the frontiers of typography and given these symbols a public immediacy that demands a completely new level of attention...

quotation from an opening
speech by Frieder Mellinghoff

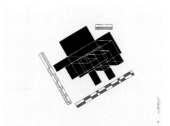

Exhibition contribution

世界デザイン博覧会　WORLD DESIGN EXPO '89
昭和64年7月15日─11月26日·名古屋　NAGOYA, JAPAN · JUL - NOV 1989

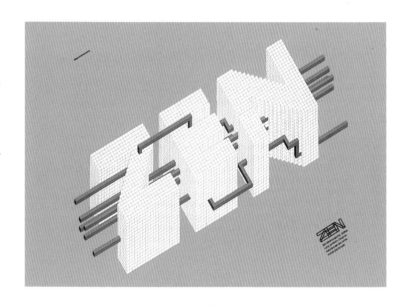

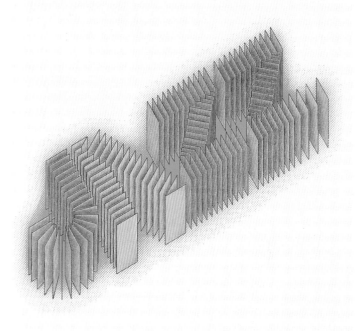

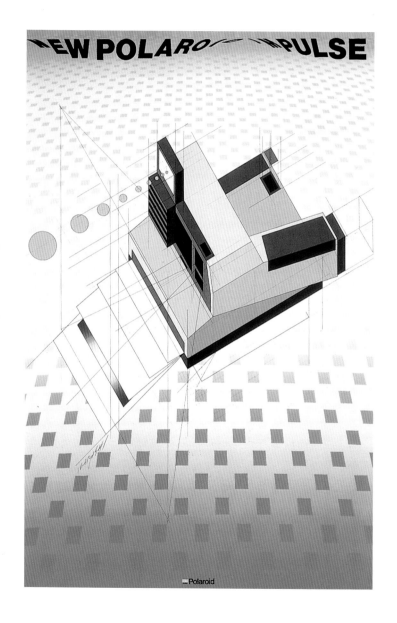

The Museum of Modern Art

TAKENOBU IGARASHI

LIVING OBJECTS

An exhibition of
modern products
and objects created
with a traditional
Japanese aesthetic

October 6–November 15, 1989
Creators Gallery
Yurakucho Seibu, Tokyo

October 11–October 18, 1989
International Design Center
New York, Center Two #210

October 25–November 18, 1989
Gallery 91, New York

November 2–December 29, 1989
Gallery of Modern Art, Los Angeles

カタチになる夢・50のプロジェクトから
五十嵐威暢展
TAKENOBU IGARASHI
50PROJECTS
8/8(火)-8/13(日)10AM-7PM(最終日は5PM)
会場・大丸藤井セントラル7F・スカイホール/札幌
TEL.011-231-1131主催・大丸藤井セントラル
企画・株式会社ディザイン/協力・株式会社
イガラシスタジオ/協賛・エー・アイ・エム株式会社
株式会社インター・オフィス、サントリー株式会社
株式会社モリサワ/CD-ROM出版・株式会社ディザイン

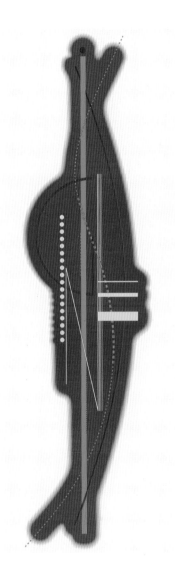

Born on the 31st March 1929 in Frauenfeld, Switzerland, Jean Widmer studied from *1946-50* at the Kunstgewerbeschule in Zürich (headed by Johannes Itten). In *1953* he settled in Paris and attended the Ecole des Beaux Arts. From *1956-69* he was Art Director of the advertising agency SNIP, the Galeries Lafayette Warehouse and the fashion magazine Jardin des Modes. He was also a professor at the Technical College for Decorative Art in Paris. Since *1969*, he has worked on corporate imaging and design strategies for national institutions, tourist information for motorways, exhibition graphics and posters for museums.

Awards: *1980* Toulouse-Lautrec Prize in Berlin, Essen and Munich for his Kiel Week poster; *1991* Officier de l'ordre des Arts et des Lettres; *1992* Distinctive Merit Award from the Art Directors Club; *1994* Grand prix national des Arts graphiques (Ministère de la Culture).

Exhibition: "Jean Widmer, graphic designer, ecologist of pictures", a one-man exhibition at the Pompidou Centre in Paris to coincide with the publication of the monograph. "Jean Widmer, un écologiste de l'image" (1995-96).

...Widmer is one of the few designers to have understood that visual communication has advanced from being a purely technical matter of interpretation into a sensually rich component of the real world and, moreover, to have played a part in developing it in relevant commissions...

quotation from the opening
speech by Friedrich Friedl

Exhibition contribution

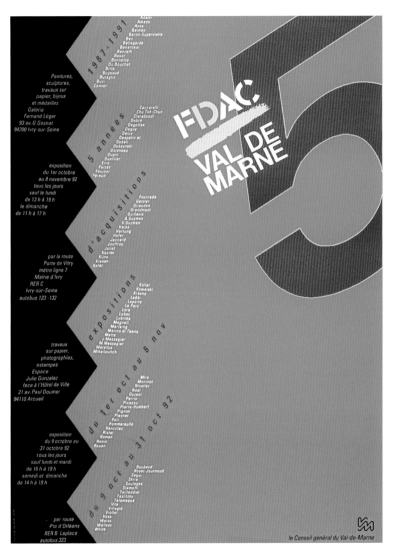

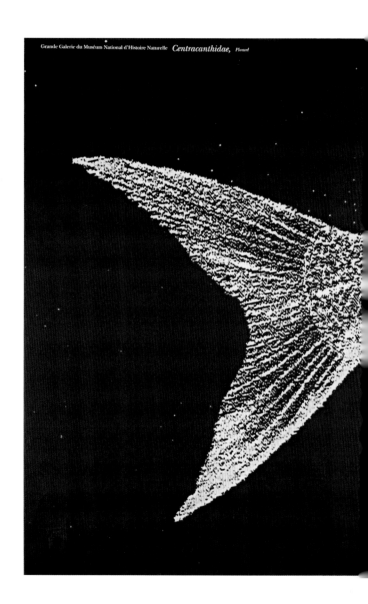

Grande Galerie du Muséum National d'Histoire Naturelle *Centracanthidae,* Picart

ouverture

rande Galerie

du Muséum National d'Histoire Naturelle

design français

centre de création
industrielle

design architectural,
industriel, intérieur,
graphique.

pavillon de marsan
palais du louvre
107 rue de rivoli, paris
22 oct. – 20 déc. 71

outillage

centre de création
industrielle

sélection internationale
outils à main, électro-
portatifs et de jardin
16 juin - 11 septembre 72

pavillon de marsan
palais du louvre
107 rue de rivoli paris 1
entrée gratuite

Fritz Gottschalk

Photo by Roddy Smith

Born December 30, 1937, Zürich, Switzerland. Founder and principal of Gottschalk + Ash International. *1954-58* apprenticeship as typographer at Art. Institut Orell Füssli, Zürich. Studied at Kunstgewerbeschule Zürich and Allgemeine Gewerbeschule Basel. In *1961-64* he received three awards for excellence from the Swiss Department of Interior. After freelancing in Paris *1959-60* and working for industry in London *1960-63* he moved to Canada. After having worked for Paul Arthur & Associates and Expo 67 he opened his own studio with Stuart Ash in *1966*. In *1975* he was juror of "Spectrum '75", the Royal Academy Art Exhibition on the occasion of the *1976* Olympic Games in Montréal. From *1976-78* he built up the G + A New York office in collaboration with Ken Carbone and Leslie Smolan, now Carbone Smolan Associates. Since his return to Zürich in *1979* he concentrates on communication design, corporate identity and architectural graphics. From *1982-89* also responsable for the Milan office in collaboration with Walter Ballmer. *1983-89* Faculty member of the Kent Summer Graphic Design Workshop in Rapperswil, Switzerland. *1985-1991* Secretary Treasurer for Alliance Graphique Internationale. *1990* Graphis Publishing, Member Board of Directors. *1991* Member Board of Trustees Coninx Museum, Zürich. Lecturer at Ohio State University, Kent State University and Yale University.

Gottschalk + Ash Int'l today consists of partners Peter Steiner and Hélène L'Heureux (Montréal), Stuart Ash (Toronto), Fritz Gottschalk (Zürich). G + A employees approx. 30 people.

...Visual communication is not just a "job". As a designer, you must respect life. The same thing goes for clients and their expectations. It may be that design begins in your head and is refind with your eyes, but what is most important is that human touch...

quotation from the opening
speech by Olaf Leu

Exhibition contribution

Ausstellung

mit französischer Druckgraphik
von Corot bis Matisse

7. September bis 17. Dezember 1995

Di – Sa 14 bis 17 Uhr
So   11 bis 17 Uhr

PEEP S HOW

oder Aspekte der optischen Wahrnehmung

CONINX MUSEUM
KUNST. SAMMLUNG. AUSSTELLUNGEN.

HEUELSTRASSE 32 CH-8032 ZÜRICH
TELEFON 0041 1 252 04 68
FAX 0041 1 252 04 68
Trägerschaft Werner-Coninx-Stiftung

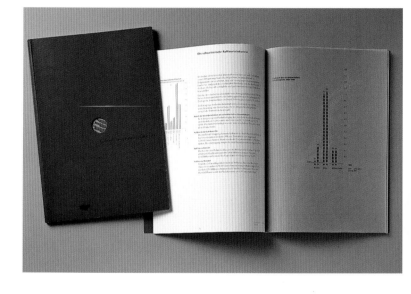

Mit Qualität in die Zukunft:
Das Plakat

Total Design

In 1998 Total Design will celebrate its 35th anniversary. The company was founded as the first multi-discipline design studio in the Netherlands. In its working rooms, interior, industrial, graphic and media designers as well as a project manager all work together. Originally the studio had been built on the reputation of the firm founders, Wim Crouwel, Friso Kramer and Benno Wissing, but little by little it got the kind of commissions which required the bundling up of all skills and disciplines. The emerging phenomen of "Corporate Design" received immediate encouragement from Total Design. Ranstadt, the SHV-Group and various Dutch Ministries all had their corporate design developed by the studio. Corporate Identity programmes still are one of the main activities of the studio (Thalys, TBI bouw).

Very early on, Total Design made use of the opportunities provided by digital data processing to facilitate the creative work of the company and it began to develop specifically in-house software. To the latest developments in the field of user software belongs the "White Office" concept, a digital corporate design with "white" stationery. This concept was first introduced at the "European Designer '96" trade fair in Maastricht.

...In its pioneering period the studio had stamped its mark "unasked" on a whole generation of its own competitors. We made the Netherlands more design conscious, and nearly all of today's famous designers have worked in our house...

quotation from the opening
speech by Olaf Leu

Galerie von Oertzen zeigt:

Total Design

Die Ausstellung ist geöffnet
vom 26. November 1991
bis zum 29. Februar 1992
Montag bis Freitag
von 9.00 bis 17.00 Uhr.

and

Dimensions

Mainzer Landstr. 250-252
6000 Frankfurt am Main

Exhibition contribution

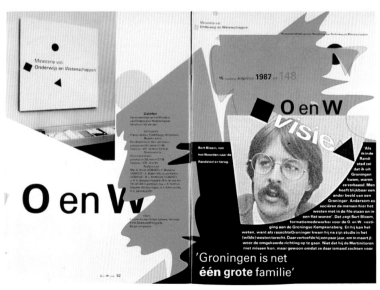

26   27

Zoals Jezus de tempel zuiverde, zo wilden velen dat met de kerk doen. Erasmus, Luther en Calvijn, doopsgezinden en rooms-katholieken probeerden dit ideaal op hun eigen wijze te bereiken.

Karel V voltooide de centralisatie van bestuur en rechtspraak in Nederland. Landvoogdes Maria van Hongarije werkte nu samen met landelijke raden en rechtbanken in Brussel en Mechelen.

Willem van Oranje
opstand tegen het
bestuur. In 1584 w
door pistoolschoten

10

Joe Duffy – Duffy Design Group

Born in Minneapolis, Minnesota, USA, Joe Duffy was educated at the Minneapolis College of Art and Design and at the University of Minnesota.
Joe Duffy is president and creative director of the Duffy Design Group, which was founded in the autumn of 1984. Their work encompasses all facets of graphic design, posters, logos, corporate identity development, even packaging.
Joe Duffy has received many awards for design and illustration from national and international design organizations, and has a number of publications to his name.
He is a member of the Board of Directors of the national AIGA and the Minnesota Department of Arts Education.

...their works amount to an aesthetic gold mine
such as is rarely discovered. There are no limits
to the wealth of forms in this style of illustration; it stretches from the old art of engraving
to modern formal graphic...

quotation from the opening speech
by H.-C. von Oertzen

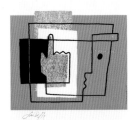

Exhibition contribution

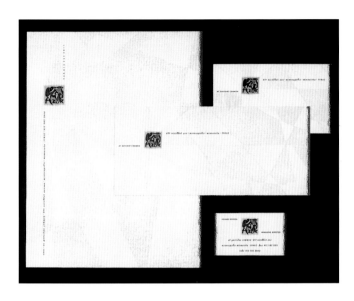

THE SNOW MAIDEN

A Fairy Tale
Opera
Rimsky Korsakov
Presented By
Philip Brunelle's
Plymouth
Music Series
February Third
Nineteen Hundred
Eighty-Nine
Seven Thirty
In the Evening
O'Shaughnessy
Auditorium
810 Ave Five
An Event Of
The St Paul
Winter Carnival
Promotions By
Mpls. St Paul
Magazine
Design By
The Duffy Design
Group

Ken Cato is an Australian designer with an international reputation. He is Chairman of Cato Design Inc., one of Australia's leading design companies, established in Melbourne 1970.

Cato's work encompasses many facets of design extending from graphic design through to product design, interior and environmental design and most recently website design.

Ken is currently President of Alliance Graphique Internationale, and his work is featured in museums and galleries worldwide. He has won numerous Australian and international design awards, and the work of Cato Design Inc. was celebrated in a 25th Anniversary exhibition.

In 1995 Ken was also awarded the first Australian Honorary Doctorate of Design from Swinburne University, and was inducted into the "Hall of Fame" of the inaugural Victorian Design Awards.

Ken is a foundation member of the Australian Writers and Art Directors Association, a member of the American Institute of Graphic Arts, ICOGRADA, the Design Institute of Australia, the Australian Marketing Institute, the Industrial Design Council of Australia, and the Australian Academy of Design.

Publications include First Choice (First and Second Editions), Design for Business, GD 3D, and Cato Design which presents a selection of the company's work from its 25-year history.

> ...Ken Cato is for me personally the founder of the Holy Roman Empire of design. His outpost on the Pacific Rim equates with the listening and trading posts of the limes. His continuing presence in publications for design generally and especially the one he is responsible for, gives him the influence of an Axel Springer...

quotation from the opening
speech by Olaf Leu

Exhibition contribution

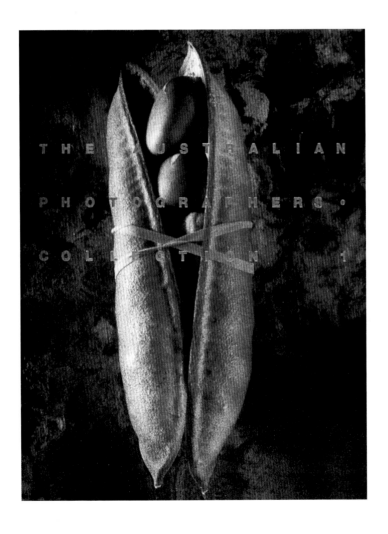

THE AUSTRALIAN

PHOTOGRAPHERS·

COLLECTION

Three Australians

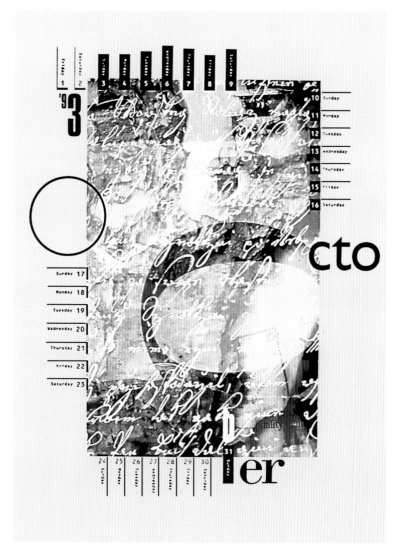

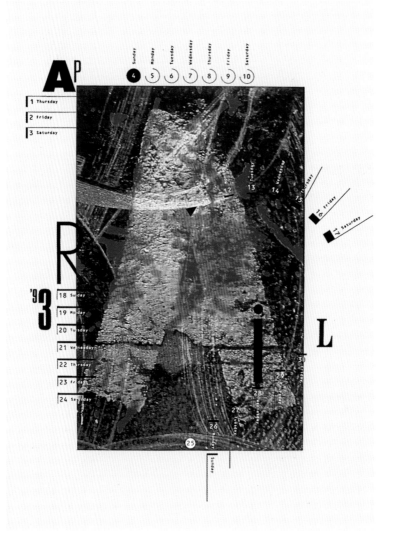

AP

'9**3**

R

L

Sunday 4
Monday 5
Tuesday 6
Wednesday 7
Thursday 8
Friday 9
Saturday 10

1 Thursday
2 Friday
3 Saturday

12
13 Tuesday
14 Wednesday
15 Thursday
16 Friday
17 Saturday

18 Sunday
19 Monday
20 Tuesday
21 Wednesday
22 Thursday
23 Friday
24 Saturday

25
26 Monday
27 Tuesday
28 Wednesday
29 Thursday
30 Friday

Sunday

Three Australians
Ken Cato, <u>Garry Emery</u>, Barrie Tucker

Garry Emery is design director of Emery Vincent Design, an Australian graphic design practice, with offices in Melbourne and Sydney. He is a member of the Alliance Graphique Internationale. Recent International awards include: the Gold Award from the Tokyo Type Director's Club, the Gold Award and Silver Award from the Biennale of Graphic Design, Brno, Czech Republic, and both the 1996 Award of Honour and Award of Merit from the Society of Environmental Graphic Design, USA.

Graphics programs have been undertaken or are in progress for many major public projects including: Parliament House of Australia, Powerhouse Museum, Australian Embassies in Tokyo and Beijing. Australian National Maritime Museum, Melbourne Exhibition Centre, Museum of Victoria, Sydney Olympics 2000, Australia Post at Expo '88, State Library of Victoria and Singapore Mega Exhibition Centre.

The practice is currently working on corporate, public and institutional projects in Australia, Japan, China, Indonesia, Singapore, Malaysia, Hong Kong, USA, Russia and Poland.

...Garry Emery is Australia's Dieter Rams. His cool, intellectual conclusions are unerring and have a timeless elegance...

quotation from the opening
speech by Olaf Leu

Exhibition contribution

| 116 |

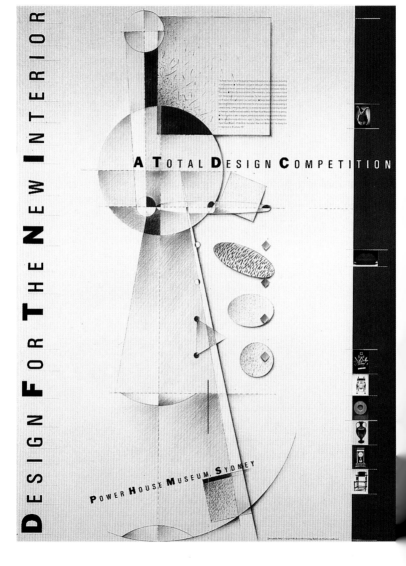

VISIONS

PETER GARRETT

FACING serious Rock FUTURE

1P

PETER GARRETT is president of the Australian Conservation Foundation, and lead singer with rock group Midnight Oil.

Three Australians
Ken Cato, Garry Emery, <u>Barrie Tucker</u>

Australian born, September 9, 1937, South Australia.
Membership: AGI (Alliance Graphique Internationale). FDIA (Fellow, Design Institute of Australia). AGDA (Australian Graphic Design Association).
Important Exhibitions of the last years:
"L'Etiquette de Vin" Exhibition, Lausanne, Switzerland, *1990*.
"The Design World of Barrie Tucker", AXIS Gallery, Tokio, Japan, *1991*.
"Three Australians", Galerie von Oertzen, Frankfurt, Germany, *1992*.
"World Peace Flag" Exhibition, Polish Pavilion, World Expo '92, Sevilla, Spain, *1992*.
"Gitanes, Silhouette" Exhibition, Georges Pompidou Centre, Paris, France, *1996*.
His works are representetd in a series of collections:
Icograda Permanent Collection, London, England. Museum of Art and Crafts, Hamburg, Germany. German Poster Museum, Essen, Germany. "People to People" collage/mural, UNESCO World Headquarters, Paris, France.
Major awards: First Prize, International Cultural Section, Lahti Poster Biennial, Finland, *1987*. 3 Gold and 2 Silver CLIO Statuettes, International Packaging, *1995, 1996* (USA). World Star Pack Award, International Packaging Awards, *1995* (England).

...Barrie Tucker is the maker of brands, the Zino Davidoff of Australia. Barrie Tucker gives us pleasure – without regret – and he communicates with the heart...

quotation from an opening
speech by Olaf Leu

Susumu Endo

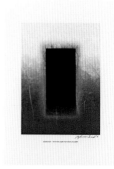

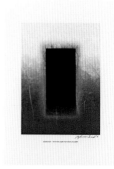

Born on the 22nd December 1933 in Kofu, Japan. Susumu Endo was educated at the Kuwasawa Design School and the Musashino Art College. In *1965* he began his career as an independent graphic designer.

Exhibitions:

Purchase Prize at International Biennial for Graphic Art, Ljubljana *1981*. First Prize at the Lahti Poster Biennial, Finland *1985*. One-man exhibition São Paulo Art Museum, Brazil *1989*. Grand-Prix at the 2nd Bharat Bhavan International Biennial of Prints, India *1991*. Grand-Prix at Interprint lviv '92, Ukraine *1992*. Special Prize at the International Triennial of Graphic Arts in Cracow *1994*. Honorable Mention at the 11th Norwegian International Print Triennial *1995*.

Susumu Endo's art is represented in several international museums:

British Museum, London / National Museum in Cracow, Poland / National Museum in Warsaw, Poland / Art Museum in São Paulo, Brazil / Ibiza Museum for Modern Art, Spain / Museum for Modern Graphic Art, Frederikstad, Norway / National Museum for Graphic Art, Kyoto, Japan / Bharat Bhavant Roopankar Museum for Graphic Art, India.

Susumu Endo has received many international awards.

> ...Endo can claim for himself that he discovered the computer as an artistic tool. He managed to produce works which previously could simply not have been created. He pointed out a new methodology for photography and photographic desig which was recognized by only a few who came after him...

quotation from the opening
speech by Olaf Leu

Exhibition contribution

EARTH CRISIS

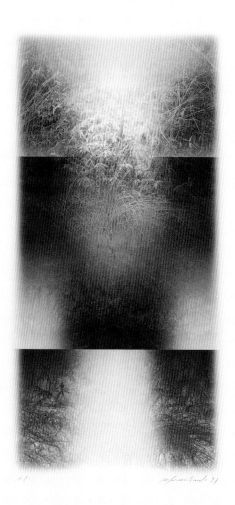

ACID RAIN CRISIS／酸性雨の危機

TAJ MAHAL in AGRA, INDIA

THE WORLD HERITAGE

世界遺産

Josse Goffin

Josse Goffin was born in Brussels November 2, 1938. Studies in graphic design at La Cambre (High School for Visual Art). Graduates in *1959* with high distinction. Works in Paris at Art Director for different publishing houses and advertising agencies. Back to Brussels in *1962*, settles down as a free-lance designer and illustrator. Since then, active in Belgian and European markets as designer for magazine cover illustration, record sleeves, children's books, TV credit titles, etc. Many cultural and commercial posters, several international advertising campaigns.

His work has been awarded many prizes and distinctions by international designer's and art directors' associations. Numerous personal exhibitions in Europe, the United States and Japan. Josse Goffin has been awarded the world's highest prize for children's books: the Grand Prix of the International Fair of Bologna, in *1991*.

Josse Goffin lives and works in Brussels where he has been teaching graphic communications at the High School for Visual Art of La Cambre since *1979*.

Fantasy and humour speak through his works whenever appropriate, while tenderness is everywhere.

...his intention is to present the complex reality of cultural and commercial life in a simple and directly understandable way...

quotation from the opening
speech by Olaf Leu

Exhibition contribution

135

Aziz Cami has more than 20 years' experience in the design industry. He was President of D&AD, Europe's premier association for design and advertising, from *1992-93*.

Aziz' work for The Partners has attracted much attention over the years. He has won over 120 awards from such prestigious UK awards bodies as D&AD (an astounding 57 awards) and the DBA Design Effectiveness Awards. US-based awards bodies The Art Directors Club and Communication Arts have also presented him with numerous prizes. In *1983* he established The Partners with four of the UK's leading graphic designers. He is currently managing partner for the organisation.

Since 1989, The Partners have been ranked as the UK's "most creative agency" in the Design Council's survey to measure agencies' performance by awards won for design effectiveness and creativity.

Some of Aziz' recent projects for The Partners include: international corporate identities for companies such as Decca International, House of Fraser, Lafarge Plasterboard, Patek Philippe, Rexam and Wedgwood; literature programmes for Générale des Eaux, NetWest Group and Freshfields; and merchandising concepts for Warner Bros. and Harrods.

...the work of this group is highly remarkable for many reasons. The "Partners" have demonstrated their creative vitality not just through one or two nice posters or record sleeves, but continuously over a period of many years. This continuity is a quality seldom found in this world of fast-changing fashions...

quotation from the opening
speech by Friedrich Friedl

Exhibition contribution

Yves Zimmerman is a graphic designer, trained at the Allg. Gewerbeschule, Basel, in Switzerland. In *1957* he worked with Will Burtin, of Visual Research and Design, and later with Ulrich Franzen, the architect, both in New York. From *1958-1960* he worked at the Geigy Chemical Corporation in Ardsley, New York, and Montreal, Canada, and in *1960* he spent a year at Geigy in Basel. In *1961* he became Art Director at Geigy in Barcelona, Spain. In *1968* he established his own studio. From *1975-1988* he worked in a shared studio, "Diseño Integral", with Andre Ricard, an industrial designer, before founding the Zimmermann Acociados S.L. in *1989*. In *1995* he received the National Design Prize from the King of Spain. For some years he has been responsible for the publishing of a series of books on design for the publisher Gustavo Gili in Barcelona. He has also been a teacher at several schools in Barcelona and given lectures and seminars at various universities in Mexico.

...I would just like to get back to the citation of the Spanish King and Queen, which (I think) I have quoted in sufficient detail, which comments on his intelligent combination of professional discipline, stemming from his Swiss roots but coupled to a Spanish sensitivity and warmth, and the wholly admirable way he deals with graphic communication...

quotation from the opening
speech by Olaf Leu

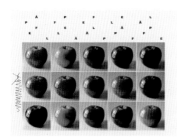

Exhibition contribution

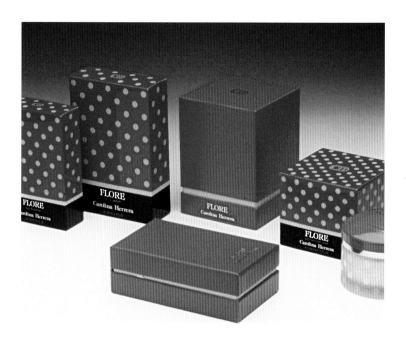

Homenaje a Federico García Lorca

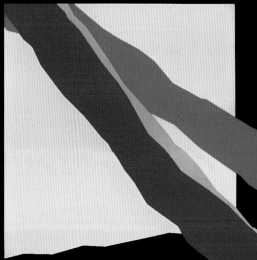

el balcón abierto

Un film de Jaime Camino

Guión de
José M. Caballero Bonald
y Jaime Camino

José Luis Gómez
Amparo Muñoz
Antonio Flores
Berta Riaza
Álvaro de Luna

Director de Fotografía:
Juan Amorós
Realización artística:
Arranz Bravo
Música: Emilio de Diego

una producción de
Tibidabo Films para
Televisión Española

Profiles

Klaus Klemp

Born in 1954 in Dortmund, Klaus Kemp studied Design & Visual Communication in Dortmund and Münster/Westf., where he took a degree in Design before going on to study Art History and History in Marburg a. d. Lahn. Now Head of the Department of Culture in the Office of Science and Art in Frankfurt a. M. and Head of Public Exhibition Halls at the Karmeliterkloster, Dr Klemp has published many books and essays on Public Design, Visual Design and the publicising of day-to-day cultural events.

Hans-Christoph von Oertzen

Hans-Christoph von Oertzen was born in Rattey, Mecklenburg, in 1917. He was educated in Potsdam and Berlin, where he completed his Abitur. Then came national service and participation in the 2nd World War, after which he studied and practised agriculture. From *1949-96* he was a publisher and the owner of a printing company. Between *1967-69* he opened the Galerie von Oertzen as a vehicle for contemporary art and in *1984* reopened it as a gallery for international graphic design. Between *1967-1997* the Galerie von Oertzen has mounted altogether 40 exhibitions.

Olaf Leu

refer to page 56

Friedrich Friedl

Friedrich Friedl was born on 7.9.1944 in Fulnek, Sudetenland/CSSR and educated in Besigheim/Neckar and Stuttgart. From *1961-1966* he worked in Stuttgart, first as an apprentice and then as a qualified typesetter. He studied Graphic Design at the Werkkunstschule in Darmstadt from *1968-72*, when he became Lecturer in Typography in the Design Faculty at the Fachhochschule in Darmstadt. In *1982* he became Professor of Typography at the Fachhochschule in Hildesheim and since *1983* has been Professor of Writing and Typography at the Hochschule für Gestaltung, Offenbach am Main. Professor Friedl has mounted many Typographic and Graphic Design exhibitions and lives in Frankfurt/M.

Frieder Mellinghoff

Born in 1941, Dr Mellinghoff is a Doctor of Philosophy and an art scholar dedicated to applied art. As Head of the Deutsches Plakatmuseum, Essen, he is involved not only in graphic design but in the whole print media culture.

Dr. Klaus Klemp

Geboren 1954 in Dortmund; Studium Design/Visuelle Kommunikation in Dortmund und Münster/Westf., Dipl.-Designer; Studium der Kunstgeschichte und Geschichtswissenschaften in Marburg a. d. Lahn.
Leiter der Abteilung Kultur des Amtes für Wissenschaft und Kunst der Stadt Frankfurt a. M. und Leiter der städtischen Ausstellungshalle Karmeliter-kloster.
Zahlreiche Buchveröffentlichungen und Aufsätze zum Public Design, zur visuellen Gestaltung und Alltagskultur.

Hans-Christoph von Oertzen

1917 geboren in Rattey, Mecklenburg, Schulbesuch in Potsdam und Berlin, Abitur, Militärdienstpflicht und Kriegsteilnahme, Landwirtschaftslehre und Praxis, *1949-96* Verleger und Druckunternehmer, *1967-69* Galerie von Oertzen für zeitgenössische Malerei, *1984-95* Galerie von Oertzen für internationales Grafik-Design.
In der Zeit von *1967-1997* wurden von der Galerie von Oertzen insgesamt 40 Ausstellungen veranstaltet.

Professor Olaf Leu

siehe Seite 56

Professor Friedrich Friedl

Geboren am 7. 9. 1944 in Fulnek, Sudetenland/CSSR. Nach Schulausbildung in Besigheim/Neckar und Stuttgart von *1961* bis *1966* Schriftsetzerlehre und Schriftsetzer in Stuttgart. *1968-1972* Grafik-Design-Studium an der Werk-kunstschule Darmstadt. *1972-1982* Dozent für Typografie am Fachbereich Gestaltung der Fachhochschule Darmstadt. *1982-1983* Professor für Typo-grafie an der Fachhochschule Hildesheim.
Seit *1983* Professor für Schrift und Typografie an der Hochschule für Gestal-tung, Offenbach am Main.
Veranstaltete zahlreiche Ausstellungen zu Typografie und Grafik-Design.
Lebt in Frankfurt/M.

Dr. Frieder Mellinghoff

Geboren 1941, Dr. phil., als Kunstwissenschaftler der angewandten Kunst verpflichtet: Als Leiter des Deutschen Plakatmuseums in Essen für Grafik-Design und die Kultur der Printmedien engagaiert.

Anton Stankowski

Geboren am 18. Juni 1906 in Gelsenkirchen. Studium an den Essener Folkwangschulen bei Max Burchartz von *1927* bis *1929*. Wird *1929* in das renommierte „Reklame-Atelier" von Max Dalang, Zürich, als Fotograf und Typograf berufen, entwickelt hier die „konstruktive Grafik". Seit *1951* eigenes Atelier in Stuttgart. *1959* Einführung des Schrägelements in die konstruktive Malerei. Ernennung zum Professor, Titelverleihung *1976* durch das Land Baden-Württemberg. *1982* Ehrengast der Villa Massimo in Rom. Anton Stankowski gründet *1983* die gemeinnützige „Stankowski-Stiftung" zur Förderung von „Kunst und Design" und gibt *1985* jeweils eine umfangreiche Stiftung von Gemälden, Grafiken und Zeichnungen an das Kunsthaus Zürich, die Staatsgalerie Stuttgart und die Kunstsammlung der Stadt Gelsenkirchen. Ausstellungstätigkeit seit *1928* im In- und Ausland. Die von ihm entworfenen Firmen-Signets und Corporate Identities prägen heute das Erscheinungsbild großer weltumspannender Unternehmen.

Oswaldo Miranda

Oswaldo Miranda (Miran), Art Director, Karikaturzeichner, Plakat-Designer und Herausgeber von Grafica Magazine, ist Gründungsmitglied des „Clube dos Diretores de Arte no Brasil", Mitglied des Type Directors Club of New York, des Art Directors Club of New York und der Alliance Graphique Internationale.

Miranda wurde mit über 450 Preisen für seine graphische Kunst ausgezeichnet, davon 75 % international. Unter den Preisen, die er in Brasilien erhielt, waren 25 Gold- und 35 Silber-Medaillen, verliehen vom Clube de Criacao de São Paulo.

In näher zurückliegender Zeit wurde Miranda *1995* mit den „Distinctive Merit Awards" auf der 74. Jahresshow des Art Directors Club of New York ausgezeichnet. Im gleichen Jahr erhielt er 4 Awards auf der International Show des TDC-Type Directors Club. In den Jahren *1991*, *1993* und *1994* wurde er mit dem Certificate of Merit and Excellence im CA-Communication Arts Annual ausgezeichnet. Zu seinem bedeutenden Rang als Grafik-Designer und Kartoonist tragen seine zahlreichen Veröffentlichungen in der internationalen Fachpresse und die vielen von ihm arrangierten Ausstellungen bei.

Professor Olaf Leu

1936 in Chemnitz geboren, aufgewachsen in Biberach an der Riß. Nach der achtjährigen Schulzeit eine dreijährige Ausbildung als Schriftsetzer *(1951-54)*. Typografischer Gestalter im künstlerischen Atelier der Bauerschen Gießerei *(1954-57)*, danach Assistent des Creative Directors in der Hanns W. Brose Werbeagentur in Frankfurt am Main *(1957-58)*. Selbständig als Grafik-Designer und Art Director *(1959-1970)*. Gründung des Studios Olaf Leu Design in Frankfurt am Main *(1971)*, das *1976* zu Olaf Leu Design & Partner wurde und bis *1991* geführt wurde. Nach dem Verkauf des Studios *1991* Konzentration auf die Gebiete der Fachpublizistik und der Lehre. Vortrags-, Seminar- und Jurytätigkeit in Europa, Süd- und Nordamerika, Indien, Australien und Neuseeland. Beteiligung an Gruppenausstellungen und 57 Einzelausstellungen. Über 310 Auszeichnungen im nationalen und internationalen Grafik-Design. Life-Member des Art Directors und des Type Directors Club of New York. Mitbegründer der grafischen Galerien in Deutschland. Lehrt seit *1986* Corporate Design an der Fachhochschule in Mainz.

153

Zdenek Ziegler

Geboren am 27. Oktober 1932 in Prag. *1943–1951* Studium, *1955–1961* an der Technischen Hochschule in Prag. Seit *1990* Lehrtätigkeit an der Akademie für Kunst, Architektur und Design. Widmet sich der Buchtypographie, der Werbegrafik, der Installierung von Ausstellungen und der freien Grafik.

Mitglied der Association Graphique Internationale. Im Wettbewerb „Das schönste Buch des Jahres" gewann er *1969, 1970, 1987, 1991, 1992, 1993, 1994, 1995, 1996* Preise und Ehrenauszeichnungen. Bei der Internationalen Plakatausstellung in Karlsbad *(1964)* erhielt er eine Ehrenauszeichnung, *1964* bekam er die Ehrenauszeichnung Typomundus und *1965* die Silbermedaille bei der Internationalen Ausstellung in Colombo. Für seine Filmplakate erhielt er in Chicago *1978* den Preis Goldener Hugo, *1982* die silberne Plakette und *1983* den Bronzenen Hugo. Ehrenauszeichnungen für Filmplakate bekam er in Prag, Helsinki, Lublin und auch bei der Ausstellung Hollywood Report *(1979)*. Im Wettbewerb „Die besten Plakate des Jahres" bekam er für die Jahre *1987/88* Ehrenauszeichnungen.

Takenobu Igarashi

Takenobu Igarashi ist ein Designer und Bildhauer von internationalem Ruf. Er ist bekannt durch
seine Plakatserien mit der räumlichen Darstellung von Alphabeten und Buchstabenformen
und durch Einkaufstaschen- und Kalenderdesign für das Museum of Modern Art in New York;
durch Corporate identity-Projekte für Suntory Limited; die „Hibiki" Skulptur im Eingangsbereich
von Suntory Hall in Tokio; einer auf 150 limitierte Skulpturen Edition für die Nissan „Infinity"
Ausstellungsräume in den USA und Produkt-Design wie für Legame cordless telephone. Seine
Arbeiten befinden sich in den Permanent Collections of the Museum of Modern Art, New York,
als auch in anderen Museen und Universitäten in der ganzen Welt.

Jean Widmer

Geboren am 31. März 1929 in Frauenfeld, Schweiz. 1946–50 Studienjahre an der Kunstgewerbe-
schule in Zürich (Leitung Johannes Itten). 1953 Niederlassung in Paris, besuchte die Ecole des
Beaux Arts. 1956–69 Art Director der Werbeagentur SNIP, der Galeries Lafayette Warenhaus, der
Modezeitschrift Jardin des Modes. Professor an der Hochschule für dekorative Künste in Paris.
Seit 1969 arbeitet er an Erscheinungsbildern und Leitsystemen für nationale Institutionen,
Touristeninformationen für Autobahnen, Ausstellungsgrafik und Plakate für Museen.
Auszeichnungen: Toulouse-Lautrec-Preis in Berlin, Essen und München für das Plakat Kieler
Woche 1980. 1991 Officier de l'ordre des Arts et des Lettres, 1992 Distinctive Merit Award of the
Art Directors Club. 1994 Grand prix national des Arts graphiques (Ministère de la Culture).
Ausstellung: „Jean Widmer, graphic designer, un écologiste de l'image", eine Einzelausstellung
im Centre Pompidou in Paris in Verbindung mit dem Erscheinen der Monographie
„Jean Widmer, un écologiste de l'image" (1995-96).

Fritz Gottschalk

Partner von Gottschalk + Ash Int'l Design Consultants
Geboren am 30. Dezember 1937 in Zürich, Schweizer Bürger, seit 1968 auch kanadischer
Staatsbürger.
1954–58 Lehre als Typograph bei Orell Füssli Graphische Betriebe AG, Zürich. Studium an der
Kunstgewerbeschule Zürich und der Allgemeinen Gewerbeschule Basel. 1961–64 erhielt er
3 awards for excellence vom Schweizer Department des Inneren. Von 1959–60 Freelancer in
Paris und von 1960–63 Arbeit für die Industrie in London, dann Übersiedelung nach Kanada.
1963–66 Paul Arthur & Associates, als Graphic Designer, Mitarbeit in leitender Position am
Projekt „Expo 67" in Montreal. 1966 Gründung der Gottschalk + Ash Ltd in Montreal mit Partner
Stuart Ash.

1972 Eröffnung des Ateliers in Toronto. *1976* Eröffnung des Ateliers in New York. *1978* Rückkehr in die Schweiz. Eröffnung des Ateliers in Zürich. *1985* Übergabe des Ateliers in New York (heute Carbone Smolan Associates). *1985–91* Secretary Treasurer for AGI (Alliance Graphique Internationale). *1986–92* Atelier in Milano. *1990* Graphis Publishing, Member Board of Directors. *1991* Mitglied des Verwaltungsvorstandes Coninx Museum Zürich, Lektor an der Ohio State University, Kent State University, Washington University und Yale University.

Gottschalk + Ash Int'l umfaßt heute als Partner Peter Steiner und Hélène L'Heureux (Montréal), Stuart Ash (Toronto), Fritz Gottschalk (Zürich). G + A beschäftigt heute rund 30 Mitarbeiter.

Total Design

Im Jahr 1998 wird Total Design sein 35jähriges Gründungsjubiläum begehen.
Total Design wurde *1963* als erstes multidisziplinäres Gestaltungsbüro der Niederlande gegründet. In den Geschäftsräumen arbeiten sowohl Innenarchitekten, Industriedesigner, Graphikdesigner, Mediadesigner und ein Projektmanagement. Das Büro baute anfänglich auf der Reputation der Unternehmensgründer Wim Crouwel, Friso Kramer und Benno Wissing auf, erhielt aber nach und nach die Art von Aufträgen, die die Bündelung aller Kräfte und Disziplinen erforderten.
Das aufkommende Phänomen „Corporate Design" erhielt von Total Design deutliche Impulse. Ranstadt, die SHV-Gruppe und verschiedene niederländische Ministerien ließen ihr Corporate Design von Total Design entwickeln. Dieser mittlerweile weitestgehend auf digitalem Wege durchgeführte Aspekt des Leistungsspektrums von Total Design zählt auch heute noch zu den Hauptaktivitäten des Unternehmens.

Bereits sehr früh hat Total Design die Möglichkeiten der digitalen Datenverarbeitung für die kreative Arbeit des Büros nutzbar gemacht und bürospezifische Software entwickelt. Die hierbei gewonnenen Erfahrungen kommen letztlich auch den Kunden des Büros zugute. Zu den aktuellen Entwicklungen auf dem Gebiet der Anwendersoftware gehört das „White Office"-Konzept, ein digitales Corporate Design mit Blanco-Briefpapier. Dieses Konzept wurde anläßlich der Messe „European Designer '96" in Maastricht vorgestellt.

Joe Duffy

Geboren in Minneapolis, Minnesota, USA.
Joe Duffy erhielt seine Ausbildung im Minneapolis College of Art and Design und in der Universität von Minnesota. Joe Duffy ist Präsident und Creative Director der The Duffy Design Group. The Duffy Design Group wurde im Herbst 1984 gegründet. Ihre Arbeiten umfaßt alle Facetten des Graphic-Designs, Plakate, Logos, Corporate Identity-Entwicklungen und Verpackungsdesign. Joe Duffy erhielt zahlreiche Auszeichnungen für Design und Illustration von nationalen und internationalen Design-Organisationen mit einer Anzahl von Veröffentlichungen.

Er ist Mitglied des Board of Directors of the national AIGA und des Minnesota Department of Arts Education.

Ken Cato

Ken Cato ist ein australischer Designer von internationalem Ruf. Er ist Chairman von Cato Design Inc., einer von Australien führenden Design Agenturen. Catos Arbeit umfaßt viele Facetten des Designs, vom Grafik Design zum Produkt Design, vom Innen- und Außenarchitektur Design, und neuerdings auch Website Design. Cato ist gegenwärtig Präsident der Alliance Graphique Internationale, sein Werk wird weltweit von Museen und Galerien ausgestellt. Er hat zahlreiche australische und internationale Designauszeichnungen. 1995 wurde Ken Cato mit dem ersten Australian Honorary Doctorate of Design von der Swinburne University geehrt. Er wurde in die „Hall of Fame", der mit dem Victorian Design Awards Ausgezeichneten, aufgenommen. Cato ist Gründungsmitglied der Australian Writers und Art Directors Association und Mitglied des American Institute of Graphic Arts, ICOGRADA, des Design Institut of Australia und der Australian Academy of Design. Seine Veröffentlichungen umfassen First Choice (First and Second Editions), Design for Business, GD 3D, and Cato Design, das eine Auswahl von Arbeiten der letzten 25 Jahre seiner Agentur bringt.

Garry Emery

Garry Emery ist Design-Direktor von Emery Vincent Design, einer australischen Grafik-Design Agentur mit Filialen in Melbourne und Sidney. Er ist Mitglied der Alliance Graphique Internationale. An internationalen Auszeichnungen erhielt er vor kurzem den Gold Award des Tokyo Type Directors Club und den Gold- und Silber-Award der Biennale für Grafik-Design in Brünn, Tschechien, und beide 1996, den Award of Honour und den Award of Merit von der Society of Environmental Graphic Design, USA. Seine Agentur wurde mit der grafischen Gestaltung vieler großer öffentlicher Projekte beauftragt: Das Parliament House von Australien, das Powerhouse Museum, die australischen Gesandtschaften in Tokio und Beijing, die Royal Melbourne Zoological Gardens, das Australian National Maritime Museum, die Australia Post at Expo '88, das Melbourne Exhibition Centre, das Museum in Victoria und das Kuala Lumpur City Centre Project, die State Library in Victoria und das Singapore Mega Exhibition Centre.
        Die Praxis der Agentur ist die ständige Arbeit an körperschaftlichen, öffentlichen und institutionellen Projekten in Australien, Japan, China, Indonesien, Singapore, Malaysia, Hongkong, USA, Rußland und Polen.

Barrie Tucker

Geboren am 9. September 1937 in Südaustralien.
Barrie Tucker ist Mitglied von AGI (Alliance Graphique Internationale), FDIA (Fellow Design Institute of Australia) und AGDA (Australian Graphic Design Association). Seine Arbeiten wurden in jüngster Zeit mit zahlreichen internationalen Preisen ausgezeichnet, wie z. B.: Erster Preis International Cultural Section, Lahti Poster Biennale, Finnland, 1987 3 Gold- und 2 Silber-CLIO-Statuetten, International Packaging, 1995 und 1996 (USA). World Star Pack Award, International Packaging Awards, 1995 (England). Gold Star Pack Award, Australian National Packaging Awards, 1994. Wichtige Ausstellungen in den letzten Jahren: „L'Etiquette de Vin" Exhibition, Lausanne, Schweiz, 1990. „The Design World of Barrie Tucker", AXIS Gallery, Tokio, Japan, Dezember 1991. „Three Australians", Galerie von Oertzen, Frankfurt am Main, 1992. „World Peace Flag" Exhibition, Polnischer Pavillon, Weltausstellung '92, Sevilla, Spanien, 1992. Gitanes, Silhouette Exhibition, Georges Pompidou Centre, Paris. Ausstellungen in Museen und Sammlungen, ICOGRADA Permanent Collection, London Museum für Kunsthandwerk, Hamburg. Deutsches Plakatmuseum, Essen. „People to People" collage/mural, UNESCO World Headquarters, Paris.

Susumu Endo

geboren am 22. Dezember 1933 in Kofu, Japan.

Ausgebildet in der Kuwasawa Design School und dem Musashino Art College.

1965 Beginn der Karriere als selbständiger Grafik-Designer.

Teilnahme an Ausstellungen und Auszeichnungen:

Purchase Preis der Internationalen Biennale für Grafische Kunst, Ljubljana, *1981*. Erster Preis der Lahti Poster Biennale, Finnland *1985*. Einzelausstellung im São Paulo Kunst Museum *1989*. Grand Prix der Bharat International Biennale of Prints, Indien *1991*. Grand Prix der Interprint Iviv '92, Ukraine, *1992*. Spezial Preis der Internationalen Triennale für Grafische Kunst, Krakau, *1994*. Ehrenhafte Erwähnung bei der 2. Norwegischen Druck Triennale *1995*.

Susumu Endos Kunst ist in einer Anzahl internationaler Museen vertreten:

British Museum, London / National Museum in Krakau, Polen / National Museum in Warschau, Polen / Kunstmuseum in São Paulo, Brasilien / Ibiza Museum für Moderne Kunst, Spanien / Museum für Moderne Grafikkunst, Frederikstad, Norwegen / National Museum for Graphic Art, Kyoto, Japan / Bhavant Bharan, Roopankar Museum for Graphic Art, Indien.

Josse Goffin

Geboren in Brüssel 1938, studierte ab *1957* an den Werkstätten für Graphik de la Cambre, graduiert *1959* mit Auszeichnung. *1964* Art Director der Agentur W. Thompson in Paris, arbeitete auch für andere Pariser Werbeagenturen und Verleger, insbesondere für die Zeitschriften Lui, Elle, Marie-Claire, Jardin des Modes, Vogue. *1962* zurück in Brüssel, läßt Josse Goffin sich als freischaffender Designer und Illustrator nieder. Seither arbeitet er für den belgischen und europäischen Markt als Designer und Illustrator von Cover-Illustrationen für Magazine, Plattencover und Kinderbücher etc. Zu seiner Arbeit gehören Plakate für Kultur und Wirtschaft und Design für verschiedene internationale Werbekampagnien. Seine Arbeit wurde mit vielen Preisen und Auszeichnungen von internationalen Fachorganisationen prämiert. Zahlreiche Einzelausstellungen in Europa, USA und Japan. Josse Goffin wurde mit dem welthöchsten Preis für Kinderbücher, dem Grand Prix der International Fair of Bologna, *1991*, ausgezeichnet. Josse Goffin lebt und arbeitet in Brüssel. Seit *1979* lehrt er Grafikkommunikation an der Hochschule für visuelle Kunst La Cambre. Phantasie und Humor sprechen aus seinen Arbeiten, doch immer ist Zärtlichkeit dabei.

Aziz Cami

Aziz Cami hat über 20 Jahre Erfahrung in der Design-Industrie. Von *1992–1993* war er Präsident der Design & Art Direction, Europas erstem Zusammenschluß für Design und Werbung. Aziz' Arbeit hat viel Aufmerksamkeit auf sich gezogen. Er gewann über 120 Auszeichnungen, unter anderem von der angesehenen britischen Design & Art Direction die erstaunliche Anzahl von 57 Preisen, und die DBA Design Effectiveness Awards. Auch in den USA wurde er von The Art Director's Club and Communication Arts mit zahlreichen Preisen geehrt. *1983* gründete er The Partners mit 4 der führenden britischen Grafik-Designern.
Seit *1989* rangieren The Partners als Großbritanniens „most creative agency" nach der Recherche des Design-Councils, das den Erfolg der Agenturen nach der Anzahl der von ihnen gewonnenen Awards für Designeffektivität und Kreativität mißt.
1956/96 Zu einigen von Aziz' in jüngster Zeit betreuten Unternehmen gehören: Decca International, House of Fraser, Lafarge Plasterboard, Patek Philippe, Rexam und Wedgwood; die Erstellung von Literaturprogrammen für Générale des Eaux, Nat West Group, Freshfields und die Entwicklung neuer Produkte für Warner Bros. und Harrods.

Yves Zimmermann

Graphiker, Ausbildung an der Allg. Gewerbeschule Basel, Schweiz.
1957 Arbeit mit Will Burtin, Visual Research and Design, und später bei Ulrich Franzen, Architekt, beide in New York. *1958–1960* Arbeit bei Geigy Chemical Corporation in Ardsley, New York und Montreal, Kanada. *1960* einjähriger Aufenthalt in Basel, bei Geigy. *1961* Art Director bei Geigy in Barcelona, Spanien. *1968* Eigenes Studio. *1975–1988* Gemeinsames Studio, „Diseño Integral", mit André Ricard, Industrial Designer. *1989* Gründung von Zimmermann Asociados S. L.
1995 Nationaler Design-Preis vom König von Spanien ausgehändigt. Ist seit mehreren Jahren verantwortlicher Herausgeber einer Serie von Büchern über Design für den Verlag Gustavo Gili in Barcelona. War Lehrer an verschiedenen Schulen in Barcelona und hat Seminare und Vorträge an verschiedenen Universitäten in Mexiko gegeben.

Impressum

Copyright

© 1997
Verlag Hermann Schmidt Mainz
and the Editors/Authors

Editors

Klaus Klemp
Olaf Leu
Hans-Christoph von Oertzen

Design

Hilger/Bernstein
Büro für Gestaltung
Wiesbaden

Translation

Estrid and Charles F. Cope

Typesetting and Lithography

von Oertzen GmbH & Co. KG
Frankfurt am Main

Printed by

Universitätsdruckerei und Verlag
Hermann Schmidt, Mainz

Published 1997 by

Verlag Hermann Schmidt Mainz
ISBN 3-87439-433-6
Printed in Germany

Deutsche Bibliothek

CIP-Einheitsaufnahme
The world of graphic design at the
Galerie von Oertzen : at the Städtische
Galerie im Karmeliterkloster,
Frankfurt/Main, from 6 September
- 5 October 1997 and at the
Deutsches Plakatmuseum, Essen,
from 26 February - 10 May 1998 /
(Klaus Klemp; Olaf Leu;
Hans-Christoph von Oertzen).
-1. Aufl. - Mainz : Schmidt, 1997
ISBN 3-87439-433-6